HOMOEOPATHY
for the HOME

This book is dedicated to Dr. Margaret Tennant-Blakeway who always protests that she is not a teacher yet has never stopped teaching and sharing.

Acknowledgements

This book would not have been possible without the help and support of very many people. We would like to thank, among many others, Dr. Fiona Anderson for writing the Danger facts, Lindsay Wagener for her lovely line drawings, Nadav for the 'Bet' meditation that initiated the process, and our families for their forbearance and loving support. We hope you will enjoy this book as much as we have enjoyed writing it and that it will prove of great benefit to you and yours.

Ruth Bloch and Barbara Lewis assert the moral right to be identified as the authors of this work.

Waiver

The authors and publishers cannot accept responsibility for any damage or injury that may arise as a result of using this book.

Photographic Credits

Back cover: Georgina Steyn/SIL (left), Christine Hart-Davies (right)
Front cover: Christine Hart-Davies/NHP (top), Craig Fraser/SIL (middle and bottom)
Page 3: Leonard Hoffmann/SIL
Page 3, 5, 15, 23, 180, 204, 213, 241: Craig Fraser/SIL

Struik Publishers
(a division of New Holland Publishing
(South Africa) (Pty) Ltd)
Cornelis Struik House
80 McKenzie Street
Cape Town
8001
www.struik.co.za

New Holland Publishing is a member of the Johnnic Publishing Group

First published in 2003

10 9 8 7 6 5 4 3 2 1

Copyright © in text 2003: Ruth Bloch and Barbara Lewis
Copyright © in line drawings 2003: Ruth Bloch and Barbara Lewis
Copyright © in published edition 2003: Struik Publishers

All rights reserved. No part of this publication may be stored in a retrieval system or transmitted in any form or by any means, electronic, mechanical, photocopying, recording or otherwise, without the prior written permission of the copyright owners.

Publishing Manager: Linda de Villiers
Editor: Annlerie van Rooyen
Senior Designer: Petal Palmer
Designer: Sean Robertson
Proofreader: Joy Clack

Reproduction by Hirt & Carter Cape (Pty) Ltd
Printed and bound by Interpak Books

ISBN 1 86872 843 9

Log on to our photographic website
www.imagesofafrica.co.za for an African experience

CONTENTS

Introduction 5

PART ONE
The history of homoeopathy 15

The theory and philosophy of homoeopathy 23

Misconceptions 38

PART TWO
Materia Medica 41

PART THREE
Ailments 109

Homoeopathy for your pets 205

Remedy and ailment cards 213

Questions and answers 241

Glossary 246

Bibliography 250

Index 253

INTRODUCTION

'The highest ideal of cure is the rapid, gentle and permanent restoration of health.'

SAMUEL HAHNEMANN

PREFACE

Dr. Ruth Bloch and Dr. Barbara Lewis have written this book for you. Between us we have 45 years experience in homoeopathic practice! We have long felt a need to empower people to take responsibility for their daily health care and any minor ailments that may arise. This is not meant to negate professional advice, but rather to help you use your health care providers more judiciously.

Homoeopathy could be applied more widely and more effectively in the home. Not only can the correct usage of homoeopathy assist wonderfully when administering first aid, but it can also prevent more serious problems from developing.

Many people live far from professional help and others travel in remote areas. It therefore makes good sense to be able to treat simple, everyday health problems. There could be some danger in not knowing your limitations either homoeopathically or medically, but we always kept this in mind while writing the book. The remedies and indications for their use comply with safety criteria that should be adhered to at all times. To guide you, a medical doctor with many years of homoeopathic practice has written the Danger facts sections. Under all circumstances, seek help if that is what your instincts and intuition tell you. If someone feels or appears to be seriously ill get professional help immediately, even in the absence of symptoms. Similarly, if you feel worried or there is no improvement **immediately obtain professional advice**.

OUR AIM WITH THIS BOOK

We strongly advise you to read this book in its entirety as this will enable you to utilize the knowledge gained in an efficient and reliable manner should any crisis arise. We have carefully selected 34 remedies for you to study and apply in most first-aid situations. These remedies form the basis of nearly all commonly encountered circumstances. Professional homoeopaths may use many hundreds of different remedies – at least 2,000 are currently available. The remedies we have chosen are well known and have been used very frequently, safely and successfully over the last 200 years. All these remedies are perfectly safe to use on babies, children, your pets and the elderly. Our aim is to give you a small number that you can learn to recognize easily and apply successfully. We have, however, also included a few extra remedies in the ailment section that are specific to certain conditions at first-aid level and have covered these in less detail. Examples are *Drosera* for paroxysmal coughs and *Staphysagria* for the emotional effects of insults. Please note that both of these remedies and most others could be applied in more serious conditions that would require professional care. We have not included information that pertains to chronic conditions as our aim is to empower you to treat first-aid conditions. In general, we have predominantly described first-aid remedies but because of the multipurpose uses of many remedies, a few constitutional remedies, known as polycrests, are included. We have chosen to highlight their acute first-aid applications.

Even though we are giving you information to treat someone at first-aid level, homoeopathy in any format is always holistic, treating the whole person. Hence any acute situation would always include the emotional responses, the physical complaints and the individual's general response to his condition. Has he become hotter, colder, weepier, more irritable, thirstier, hungrier, more sweaty, and so on?

USE OF HOMOEOPATHIC NOMENCLATURE

Homoeopathy, like all other disciplines, has its own 'language'. For example, someone could be described as a typical *Rhus tox*, meaning that the symptoms displayed by the person correspond to the symptom picture of this remedy. As another example, you will come across sentences such as: 'Objective symptoms like a flushed, red face or a wet, slimy tongue are as important as subjective symptoms such as a weepy mood (*Pulsatilla*) or the sensation of a bursting pain (*Belladonna*).' In this instance it means that *Pulsatilla* should be used to treat someone in a weepy mood, and *Belladonna* would be good to treat bursting pain. You could also read about a '*Belladonna* picture', which basically refers to the symptoms that *Belladonna* can cause and therefore cure. We have also included a glossary on pages 246–250, explaining some of the homoeopathic terms used in the book.

HOW TO USE THIS BOOK

> **This book is set out in three major sections:**
> 1. The history, theory and philosophy of homoeopathy
> 2. Remedy pictures
> 3. Ailments to be treated

Resist the temptation to read only the ailments and remedy chapters. It is important that you understand the theory and principles underlying homoeopathy. Once you recognize the remedy pictures, you will be able to apply them easily and effectively.

A **remedy picture** is a description of the symptoms that form the Materia Medica of homoeopathy. The term Materia Medica is used to describe the collection of symptoms, or a précis of these symptoms, produced during a proving (*see* page 27). To this is added toxicological and clinical symptoms from cases cured by a remedy. It is a record of what can be caused and therefore cured by a remedy that is homoeopathic to the case. Perceiving the different remedy pictures and differentiating between them is one of the fascinating parts of studying and applying homoeopathy. You need to match the gestalt of a sick person to that of a remedy. An analogy is that of a bird-watcher who needs to distinguish between different birds. It is easy to tell the difference between an ostrich and a canary, but harder to see the differences between a falcon and a hawk in flight. Bright plumage will stand out as clearly as a 'strange', 'rare' or 'peculiar' symptom (*see* page 31) in a remedy picture.

The different medicines, or remedies as they are called in traditional homoeopathy, all have their own specific picture. It is our intention that you learn a small number of pictures well, so that you can apply them in many first-aid situations. Your success will depend on how well you learn to use the information given to you in matching the symptom picture of the sick person to the symptom picture of the remedy.

The remedy pictures (Materia Medica) have been set out as follows:
First, the **name** of each remedy is given, for example:
- **Aconitum napellus** (*Aconite*)
  Monkshood
- **Aconitum napellus** is the remedy's specific name, *Aconite* is the name by which the remedy is commonly known and used in homoeopathy, and monkshood is its common English name. The remedies are presented alphabetically for ease of reference.
- The **source facts** describe the origin of the remedy, which can derive from mineral, animal or vegetable matter.
- The **chat facts** provide interesting information that will help you to understand the remedy.
- The **key facts** section supplies the essential points of each remedy as they are used in acute or home situations. Please note that all the symptoms **do not** have to be present in order to prescribe. Three clear symptoms in the sick person and in the remedy will suffice. Unequivocal symptoms are highlighted in **bold** (*see* also page 32 for the discussion on complete symptoms).

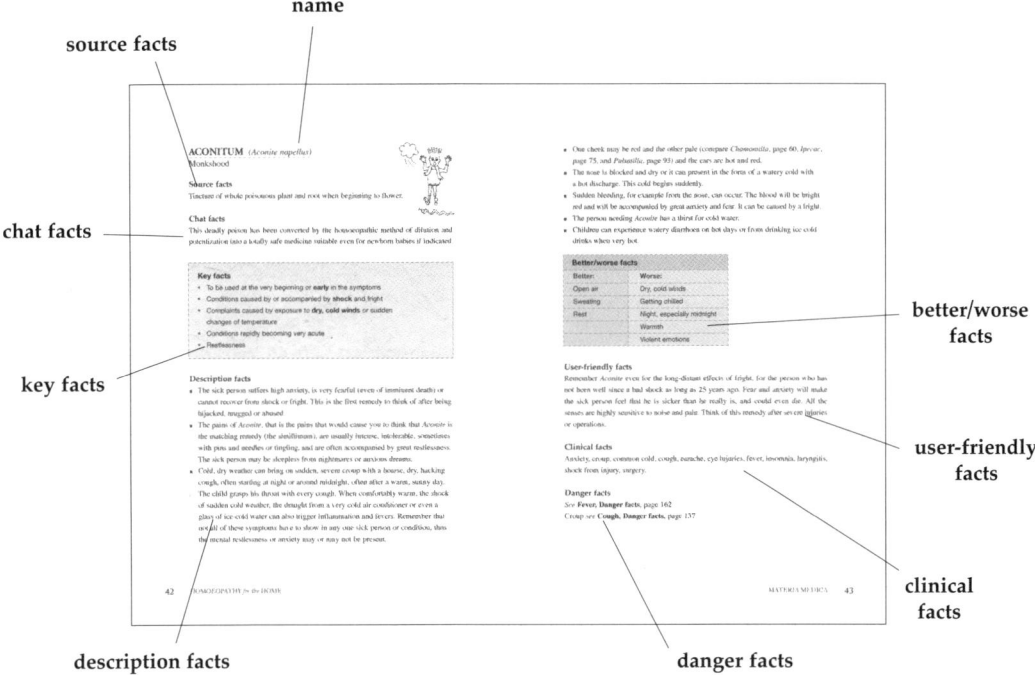

- The **description facts** are our attempt to show how the **key facts** would be applied in a real-life situation. As teaching examples, we have written some caricatures, designed to help you understand the multiple applications of a remedy. These stories obviously contain very full and exaggerated pictures and in real life you may be presented with only a few strong, clear symptoms on which to base your choice of remedy. Many other scenarios could also apply.
- The **better/worse facts** are also known as 'modalities' (*see* page 32) and are unique to homoeopathy. These are the symptoms that show how the remedy reacts individually and need to be matched in some aspect to how the sick person reacts. As an example, someone needing *Bryonia* will have the symptom, modality or 'worse for fact' of being worse from any movement. On the other hand *Rhus tox* will have the 'better for fact' of improving through movement, both in the remedy picture and in the sick person. You frequently have to choose between these remedies when treating the aches and pains of flu.

- In the **user-friendly facts** section, we have tried to indicate the 'highlights' of the remedy picture.
- The **clinical facts** list some of the conditions in which a particular remedy might prove to be useful. This information must eventually be co-ordinated with your symptom notes and cards (*see* below), for example coughs, fevers, and so on.
- The **danger facts** section has been written to make sure that you always stay within the parameters of a home help book, and remain safe.

The ailment section deals with the application of the remedies to conditions you may encounter at home, for example bleeding, bruises, colds, food poisoning, teething problems, and so on. Again the information is presented in alphabetical order. It summarizes the most useful parts from the general remedy description for use in particular homoeopathic first-aid situations. It should be read in conjuction with the remedy section, and is divided into:

- Short descriptions of the **ailments**.
- The **danger facts**, which highlight those conditions that should be treated professionally, and, as in the remedy section, helps you to stay within the parameters of this book.

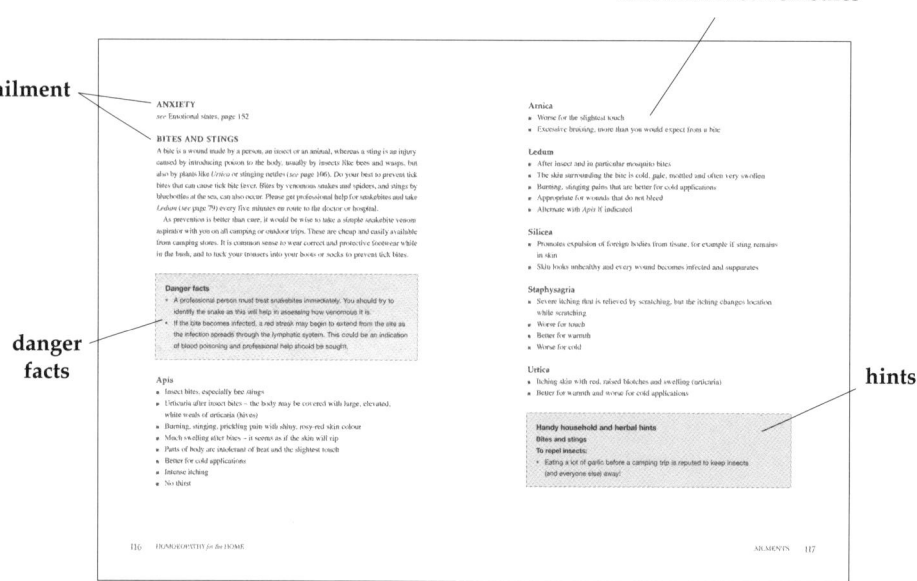

- Recommended **remedies** to treat the various ailments.
- **Handy household and herbal hints** under each ailment, giving you useful, simple alternatives with which to treat first-aid conditions.

The user-friendly **cards** have been included as a handy summary of and a quick reference to both remedies and ailments. Photocopy and laminate these cards, and keep them in alphabetical order with your first-aid remedies and book. With use, you will soon be able to recognize the pertinent facts and become skilled in remedy choice.

IN CONCLUSION
If you find that a particular condition recurs frequently, it may well indicate that a constitutional treatment and remedy would boost the immune system and alter the susceptibility of the individual. In this case, professional homoeopathic help would make a significant difference to a person's health and wellbeing.

We can't reiterate enough that the more you know, the more effective you will become. We would also like to suggest that you revise the material from time to time – don't wait for a crisis and then try to read the notes. The multiple-choice questions, drawn from real-life situations that you may encounter, will help you to test yourself and integrate this knowledge.

Homoeopathy for the Home is just the beginning of your homoeopathic adventure – enjoy it! A book list is supplied for further reading and study.

> *'... one must clearly realize what is to be cured in each single case of disease; clearly realize what is curative in each particular medicine; clearly match what is curative in the medicine to the disease in the patient according to clear principles.'*
>
> SAMUEL HAHNEMANN

PART ONE

the HISTORY, THEORY and PHILOSOPHY of HOMOEOPATHY

the HISTORY of HOMOEOPATHY

'The purpose of maintaining the body in good health

is to make it possible for you to acquire wisdom.'

MAIMONIDES

THE STORY OF DR. SAMUEL HAHNEMANN –
founder of the homoeopathic system of medicine

Samuel Hahnemann was born in the spring of 1755 in Meissen, Germany. He was a brilliant student with a flair for languages. As a medical student at the University of Leipzig he employed his genius in languages to support himself financially. He taught German and French, and translated books (mainly on the subjects of medicine, botany and chemistry) from languages such as English, Latin and Greek into German.

He then set up a practice in a small copper mining village. As a sensitive person and a humanitarian, the young doctor was soon disillusioned by his profession. Medicine in his day consisted largely of blood-letting – either in the form of venesection (lancing of veins) or by the application of leeches. Copious withdrawal of blood was a dominant feature of contemporary medical practice in the eighteenth, nineteenth and earlier part of the twentieth centuries. Venesection was generally considered necessary until the patient fainted from loss of blood. Physicians who firmly believed that it would enhance their state of wellbeing, for example, would subject pregnant women to venesection. Patients that survived the leeches and venesection were then subjected to other forms of body purging like depleting enemas, powerful laxatives, potent emetics to induce vomiting, and huge doses of strong medicines, often with horrendous side effects.

Hahnemann's horror of the brutality and barbarism of the medical profession of his day appalled him to the extent that he did not practise much medicine, but rather continued his studies of medicine and chemistry by reading and translating books, manuscripts and journals into German. On being asked why he practised so little medicine his reply was generally that he was too conscientious a person to prolong illness or make it appear more dangerous than it actually was! He also contributed to the literature of his time by writing books and articles on medicine and chemistry. In his first essay he recognized the need for hygiene, correct diet, fresh air and exercise.

Hahnemann expressed these opinions 60 years before any sort of germs were discovered and was clearly ahead of his time in his belief of a 'contagious element'. He was also the author of the *Pharmaceutical Lexicon*, a four-volume work that proposed basic guidelines and standards to which pharmacies should adhere. Concepts such as preparing medicines only from fresh, clean plant material and keeping poisons under lock and key were included in this work. The *Apothecaries Lexicon* quickly established itself as the standard reference work of the apothecaries, or pharmacies, of the time. Many of these basic precepts set down by Hahnemann are now incorporated in the provisions of the Medicines Act, which still governs the quality controls of manufacture today. Besides hygiene and a sensible lifestyle, Hahnemann advocated humanitarian treatment for the mentally ill.

At the age of 28, Dr. Samuel Hahnemann married Johanna Henriette Küchler. They were married for 49 years until her death in 1830 and had 11 children, of whom nine survived infancy.

THE BIRTH OF HOMOEOPATHY

In 1780 an event occurred which many people credit as the birth of homoeopathy. Hahnemann was commissioned to translate into German *A Treatise on Materia Medica* by Dr. William Cullen, a Scottish physician. In this book Dr. Cullen mentioned Peruvian bark that was used by the indigenous South Americans to treat malaria. The bark had been named Cinchona after the Duchess Cinchon, vice queen of Peru, who had been cured by it. The active ingredient of Cinchona bark is *China*, or quinine, used to treat malaria. Hahnemann experimented by taking small amounts of the bark extract twice a day and recorded the symptoms he experienced. He discovered that for two to three hours after he took the bark, he developed malaria-like symptoms. These symptoms included fever, drowsiness, thirst, a fast, strong pulse, heart palpitations, flushed cheeks, intolerable anxiety and trembling, and prostration of the limbs. Hahnemann thus deduced that Peruvian bark is curative in malarial fever because it can produce similar symptoms in people not suffering from malaria. This was the birth of the first basic principle of homoeopathy – Like cures like (*Similia similibus curentur*).

In order to determine the effects different substances would have on the healthy body, Hahnemann conducted experiments that later became known as provings (*see* page 27 for more detail on provings).

In 1810 the first edition of *The Organon* was published. This work is the most complete explanation of Hahnemann's system of healing. It encompasses about 20 years of painstaking and arduous experimentation, study and insight.

In this book, Hahnemann outlines various homoeopathic principles. He also explains how the medicines are prepared. Some of the remedies in their crude form are highly toxic and thus had to be diluted. Each dilution successively reduces the size of the dose, that is the quantity of crude material in the dose. In his experimentation he violently shook up the vials of medication. It has been shown by Nuclear Magnetic Resonance experiments and clinical research that dilution and violent shaking, a process called succussion, increases the efficacy and potential strength of a medication. This led to the paradox of increased strength of reaction and increased dilution of the dose. Medicines produced in this way are called **potencies** (*see* page 28). A process of serial dilutions and succussions makes different strengths of remedies.

Another important principle outlined is that of individual and holistic prescribing. The physician prescribes by the study of the whole person. The person is treated, not just the disease. In Hahnemann's opinion, only the most careful observer can become a true scientific healer.

The Hahnemann family did a lot of travelling in their lives, often moving from one city to another. There were many reasons for their nomadic lifestyle: the war, new career opportunities, and antagonism to his new methods and ideas.

Hahnemann wrote to Duke Ferdinand, ruler of Anhalt-Kothenasking, asking his permission, at the age of 66, to settle and practise in Kothen, a small autonomous central German principality. The duke, who was his patient, was happy to comply and the following article appeared in the local newspaper:

> **PUBLIC RECOGNITION OF HAHNEMANN**
>
> The inventor of the homoeopathic system, Dr. Samuel Hahnemann, leaves Leipzig in the next few days, and will establish himself as a practising physician in Kothen. His Serene Highness, the Duke of Anhalt-Kothenasking, has not only allowed him to do this, but also graciously granted him permission to prepare with his own hands the required medicines and dispense them himself to his patients, without the intervention of the apothecaries. The Medical Council of Kothen has given by this act a praiseworthy example of impartiality and of true regard for the progress of science... Dr. Hahnemann can hardly be forbidden the right for preparing and dispensing his own medicine in view of the fact that for 20 years the apothecaries of Germany have consulted his *Apothecaries Lexicon* whenever in doubt... a large number of patients whose treatment was interrupted for several months because of the persecution against Dr. Hahnemann will now be able to follow their own inclinations unmolested and our free-thinking century is spared the reproach of having suppressed one of the most remarkable discoveries for the welfare of humanity.

Hahnemann's practice thrived in Kothen and his life there was relatively uneventful until the death of his wife of 49 years when he was 77. A few months after his wife's death, a cholera epidemic swept through Western Europe. Homoeopathic treatment of the disease proved to be remarkably successful as opposed to the allopathic treatment that consisted of bloodletting. Only a few of the cholera patients treated homoeopathically died, while almost 50 per cent of those treated allopathically did not survive. Reports from the rest of Europe showed similar results.

A new start in Paris

In 1834, Mademoiselle Marie Melanie d'Hervilly, a 30-year-old artist from a wealthy family, came from Paris to consult with Hahnemann. She immediately caused a stir in Kothen as she was wearing what was described as 'man's attire'! In Paris it was fashionable for women to dress in trousers and especially sensible for a woman travelling alone for purposes of safety. In nineteenth-century Germany, however, before the emancipation of women, her attire caused considerable shock and consternation. Her arrival certainly did not go unnoticed!

Melanie held strong views on the fact that women were prevented from entering professions such as medicine. Samuel Hahnemann, almost 80 years of age, was instantly attracted to her and the feeling was mutual. To his daughters' horror they were married after a few weeks.

To the delight of the French homoeopathic community, the honourable founder of homoeopathy then accompanied his wife to Paris where they established a practice and started a new life.

'It is absurd to view disease as separate from the living whole being.'

SAMUEL HAHNEMANN

'All medicines alter the mental and emotional state, each in a different way.'

SAMUEL HAHNEMANN

> *'In health, the life force keeps all parts of the organism in harmony. Without the immaterial life force, the material organism is dead. In disease, the life force is dynamically out of tune and manifests this through symptoms.'*
>
> SAMUEL HAHNEMANN

Hahnemann's skill as a homoeopath combined with Melanie's charm and ambition proved to be a remarkable combination. By the late 1830s their practice had become the most celebrated in Europe. The Hahnemanns treated members of all walks of life – from kings and dukes to the poorest of the poor – employing his lifelong custom of charging according to a sliding scale. Hahnemann confided to a friend in a letter that his final years in Paris were the happiest of his life. He felt younger and healthier than ever before despite long working hours and an active social life.

Dr. Samuel Hahnemann died peacefully in his sleep at the age of 88.

Although Melanie must have realized that Hahnemann was not immortal and that she would outlive him by a great number of years, she was grief-stricken by his death. The only way she could cope with her profound pain was to carry out her husband's last wishes to honour their sacred trust. This trust was to continue the practice of homoeopathy the way Hahnemann had developed it. It was no secret that Hahnemann had considered Melanie to be the finest homoeopath in Europe and that he had trusted her implicitly with their patients.

For two years after Hahnemann's death, Melanie continued her practice, making her the first woman to practice homoeopathy. Inevitably, the success she achieved in her own right stirred up animosity among the medical profession. It is difficult to establish whether the prejudice displayed by the medical profession had been directed against the intrusion by a woman into their 'all male' domain, or whether it was against unqualified medical practitioners. The fact remained, however, that while practising medicine as a woman was not against the law, practising medicine while unqualified was! Although Melanie had obtained a diploma in homoeopathy from an American college, her qualification was not recognized in France. It was only 20 years later that women were even allowed to enter universities. In 1847, the courts forbade Melanie to practice homoeopathy until 1872 when her American diploma was finally recognized. At the age of 72, Melanie Hahnemann finally became a qualified homoeopath!

Six years later, she succumbed to an illness and was laid to rest in the grave next to her beloved Samuel, the same place that she had constantly visited over the years to read the inscription on Hahnemann's grave: *Non inutilis vixi* – I have not lived in vain.

the THEORY and PHILOSOPHY of HOMOEOPATHY

'The most appropriate medicine for a given case of disease is the one that is the most homoeopathically selected and which is administered in the correct dose.'

SAMUEL HAHNEMANN

WHAT IS HOMOEOPATHY?

The word homoeopathy is derived from the words *homoios* meaning 'similar' and *pathos* meaning 'suffering'. But the giving of a similar medicine to treat illness is ancient and predates homoeopathy. Hippocrates (470 B.C.), the father of modern medicine, stated that illness could be treated by similars, contraries or by substitution. An example of cure by similars is taking a drink to 'cure' a hangover. The hair of the dog that bit you! Putting ice on a burn is an example of contraries, while using insulin in the treatment of diabetes explains the principle of substitution.

THE LAW OF SIMILARS

What does it mean to give a similar medicine? The common onion illustrates this well. If you are sensitive to it, your eyes will stream and burn and your nose will run as you chop an onion. From this example, it is clear that an onion can cause symptoms such as a runny nose and burning, runny eyes and can therefore be used to treat a similar condition like a cold or hay fever, which displays these specific symptoms. This is a description of a scientific homoeopathic principle called 'The Law of Similars'. Even in our modern conventional medicine some drugs fall into this category. For instance, Ritalin is used to calm down hyperactive children but can have a stimulating effect in normally active children and in adults. It is also well known that radiation can cause cancer but can also be used to treat it. The treatment using similars is best expressed by homoeopathy's motto – Like cures like (*Similia simillibus curentur*). In other words the application of the Law of Similars means that the remedy for any individual illness is the very substance that can produce a similar symptom picture and pattern of the illness.

Until the eighteenth century, the principle of similars could not be applied because the methodology was lacking. For a system of medicine to be acceptable, it must be reproducible in a reliable manner. In other words, you should be able to study homoeopathy and apply the knowledge and not have to guess or intuit the application.

The genius of Samuel Hahnemann, the founder of homoeopathy, was that he developed the methodology that made the application of the principle of similarity possible, safe and effective.

The Organon is the basic textbook of his system. He reformulated and rewrote six upgraded editions in his lifetime. In paragraph 2 of his *Organon of Healing* he states, 'The highest ideal of therapy is to restore health rapidly, gently, permanently; to remove and destroy the whole disease in the shortest, surest, least harmful way, according to clear, comprehensible principles.'

Homoeopathy, as a science and an art, has continued to expand and grow over the last 200 years. Lately there has been an expansion of research, an inclusion of many new remedies and an integration of modern psychology, modern diagnostic medicine, computer-assisted analyses and in-depth training of professional homoeopaths all over the world. Although we are not yet completely sure of how homoeopathy works, it seems from current research that the answers lie in the realm of modern quantum physics and not in the old-style chemistry and molecular paradigm.

AN ALTERNATIVE APPROACH

First and foremost, homoeopathy is a system of medicine and an alternative approach to treating illness. In certain circumstances, it can be used to complement conventional medicine, for example surgery, acute trauma and overwhelming infections. It is also complementary to psychotherapy. Homoeopathy, being holistic in concept, utilizes dietary changes, vitamin therapy, herbalism, psychotherapy, or whatever may be necessary in an individual case. Nevertheless, its holistic approach does not consist of putting together a vast number of different treatments. Instead it stems from the idea that each individual will both experience and display her illness characteristically and individually and that there will be a specific medicine with a similar pattern to treat that specific person with her specific suffering. In other words, we ask not only 'what' a person suffers but 'who', 'what' and 'how' she suffers?

An example of a simple headache will make this concept clearer. A person who will require the

> *'Even a few symptoms shared by a medicine and a disease can lead directly to a cure if the symptoms are characteristic.'*
>
> SAMUEL HAHNEMANN

remedy *Bryonia* for a headache will be irritable, bad-tempered and want to be left alone to lie quietly and not move the head or even the eyes. Even the effort of thinking or talking will make the sufferer feel worse. The pain is described as bursting or stitching and will improve by applying hard pressure or lying on the sore area. There will be an intense thirst for large quantities of cold water.

In contrast, the person requiring *Pulsatilla* for a throbbing headache will have no thirst in spite of a dry mouth and will feel restless. She will feel better if she walks around slowly in fresh air. She will be in a weepy or vulnerable mood and will feel sensitive. Company and comfort will help the *Pulsatilla* patient.

What can be concluded from this? The headache is common to both headache sufferers, but the emotional and physical reactions are individual. In homoeopathy we need to prescribe remedies that are similar not only to headaches but to the whole individual and personal reaction. To reiterate, this is an example of the homoeopathic individual holistic concept that is relevant in both acute and chronic disease. It illustrates clearly that homoeopathy rests firmly on the foundation of individual reaction, which leads us to understand that person's individual susceptibility.

WHAT IS SUSCEPTIBILITY?

We are born with weak or strong constitutions. For example, one person can eat and live incorrectly, ignoring all common-sense health knowledge and yet never get ill, while another has to take good care to remain in good health. A person with a weak constitution is easily susceptible to becoming ill. In a flu epidemic, as another example, not everyone contracts flu. Often fatigue, poor nutrition, emotional distress, and so on, will lower the resistance of the person, thus making her susceptible 'to catch the flu'. Illness is therefore never unconditional – there has to be a degree of susceptibility. We are all susceptible to our sensitive spots. For instance, a little sugar upsets those who are intolerant of it; and a bee sting can prove fatal if you are allergic and susceptible to being stung. If a person is allergic to roses, the roses do not have to be on his desk to provoke a reaction. The roses only have to flower in the neighbourhood and the sufferer will sneeze throughout the summer. Hence susceptibility embraces reactivity and sensitivity.

Susceptibility is the degree of vulnerability to becoming ill. It is that which needs to be treated by the constitutional prescription in order to prevent or retard the occurrence of acute manifestations of chronic illness. We can elaborate on this with an example of 'migraine headaches'. The acute headache could be treated with the knowledge gained from this book, but to stop the recurrence of the migraines, the underlying chronic problem requires a more profound constitutional prescription. Treating the underlying weaknesses of a constitution is unique to homoeopathy and can help build up the individual's wellbeing, strength and resistance to illness. This constitutional type of prescribing is very complex and must be undertaken by professional homoeopaths only.

The characteristic reaction patterns of the remedies are explained clearly in the Materia Medica or remedy picture section (*see* pages 41–107). This will help you to find the specific remedy that is similar both to the illness and to the personal, characteristic reaction of the sick person. This person has to be susceptible to the remedy to react in a curative manner. We then say that the prescription was 'homoeopathic' to the individual and to her manner of suffering.

PROVINGS

To discover the curative value of medicines, homoeopathy utilizes a unique system called provings. Provings are best illustrated by Samuel Hahnemann's famous experiment with *China*, or quinine (*see also* page 17). Hahnemann deduced that Cinchona bark is curative in malarial fever because it can produce similar symptoms in healthy people. This was the birth of the first basic principle of homoeopathy – Like cures like (*Similia similibus curentur*). In order to determine what effects different substances would have on the healthy body, Hahnemann conducted experiments that later became known as **provings**. In these experiments he would test small amounts of the carefully prepared substance first on himself and then on other volunteers. The **provers** included members of his family, friends and his followers – medical practitioners who preferred his homoeopathic system of healing. Hahnemann would meticulously note and record every sign shown, and every symptom experienced, by the provers. In this way the various **remedy pictures** were created.

Over the years it has been verified that if remedies in potentized form (*see* page 28) are given to a group of healthy provers, certain predictable events will take place. In any group only some provers will be sensitive or susceptible to the medicine being proved. They will develop proving symptoms in certain areas of their being, whether emotional or physical. It takes many repeated provings of people of both genders and all ages to elicit the full proving picture. A remedy is fully proven when we have discovered all the symptoms that that remedy can produce in the emotions, thought processes and in the body. The proving picture becomes the Materia Medica or drug picture of the remedy. As this remedy is used and found to heal sick people in a reliable way, more clinical symptoms are added to the picture.

The symptoms of overdosing of the crude herb or material are also considered to be of importance to the remedy picture and are called toxicological symptoms. For example, sulphur in crude doses can cause some people to have side effects such as boils and an itchy rash or diarrhoea. These people are sensitive to the 'sulphur illness', and these symptoms are therefore very useful to include in the drug picture. Sulphur as a potentized homoeopathic remedy can cure certain types of skin rashes and diarrhoea in sick people. Because some of the substances are poisonous, provings are always undertaken with diluted and potentized material, which is completely safe.

A system of provings to elucidate the healing potentials within substances was one of Hahnemann's major contributions to experimental medical science. He was the first person to study the effects of medicine on human beings. Today we continue our tests along the lines Hahnemann suggested. Only healthy volunteers are chosen of both genders and various ages. Their health is assessed and recorded as a baseline for the experiment. Some of these volunteers are given a potentized remedy repeatedly and others are given placebos repeatedly to ensure impartiality. This is called a 'double blind' trial.

There are a few important points to be emphasized here:
- the remedy is given to healthy people who do not need the medicine
- the potentized remedy and not the crude substance is used in the proving
- control groups are used to ensure impartiality
- these provings are reproducible and therefore scientific and reliable.

POTENCIES

Potencies are highly diluted, energized substances prepared according to specified and standardized pharmaceutical methods, and made according to worldwide guidelines. Herbs, minerals, metals and some animal products are used to produce homoeopathic preparations. The range is very diverse and new remedies are constantly being researched, proven and introduced into our Materia Medicas and our clinical practices. Although the old remedies are not discarded, we are constantly seeking specific remedies for the myriad ills of our modern society.

In the example of the person who is allergic to roses, we emphasized how highly sensitive a susceptible person is to what will make him sick. If it were decided to treat this person with rose extract, the reaction might be very severe. If the rose extract were diluted and made into a potency, the person would be able to tolerate this minute dose that has been converted into a gentle, highly effective, specific treatment.

The advantage of these potencies is that they will make even the most toxic product **perfectly safe, even for the pregnant mum and newborn baby**. Yet these specially prepared dilutions are very effective and powerful, without any side effects.

Manufacture of potencies

To prepare remedies, soluble substances are extracted in an alcohol and water mixture. This herbal tincture is the source material and is not yet a homoeopathic potency. This tincture is further diluted in an alcohol and water mixture, and immediately after dilution, potentization takes place. It is achieved by shaking the bottle containing the tincture vigorously for a specified number of times, a process known as succussion (*see also* page 17). In Hahnemann's times, the bottle was banged against a leather-bound book. It would appear from research in modern quantum physics that this process of vigorous shaking transfers kinetic energy into the substance. Recent research also seems to indicate that the inner chemical bond of water molecules is able to imprint the memory of the substance undergoing succussion. In other words, the pattern of the substance seems to be imprinted on the water/alcohol mixture. Hahnemann believed and experience has borne out the fact that potentization is of the utmost importance in making homoeopathic remedies effective. This repeated dilution and succussion is continued until the desired potency or **strength** is achieved.

Insoluble substances are 'triturated' in lactose (milk sugar). Potencies are made by placing the substance in lactose in the required ratio and then grinding it for many hours, using a mortar and pestle. This process of grinding is called trituration and is the equivalent of shaking or succussion when manufacturing soluble substances.

Three different scales of potency are currently used

- The original scale, first developed by Hahnemann, was the centesimal scale. At each step of manufacturing as described above, the remedy is diluted 100 times, and succussed for its specified number of times. Each repetition raises the potency (strength) by 1ch. The 'c' stands for centesimal and the 'h' for the Hahnemannian method, using separate bottles. A 6ch potency, for example, has been diluted and succussed six times.
- The decimal scale was introduced by Dr Hering who spent many years in the jungles of South America proving indigenous materials. With this scale the

substance is diluted one part in 10 at each step of the manufacturing process, followed by succussion. It is indicated by a 'd' meaning decimal or 'x', the Roman 10.
- The 50 millesimal or LM potency scale was developed by Hahnemann in his last and 6th edition of *The Organon*. This is a more complex method of dilution and succussion and is used mainly by professional homoeopaths.

The potencies made are then used to saturate tablets, granules, powders or low percentage alcohol. As can be seen, there is a major difference between homoeopathically prepared substances and the original tinctures or material from which they are made. In homoeopathy, a remedy will be chosen according to its similarity to the sick person's symptom picture. A herbal remedy is chosen for its chemical, pharmacological potential in treating an ailment.

Repertories

The symptoms of provings are analyzed and collated and a remedy picture becomes apparent. Collated symptoms are written into repertories. A **repertory** is a book listing all the symptoms that have been elicited during a proving as well as clinical verifications. Repertories vary in size and detail. The larger repertories contain the remedies in a graded format as well as references to the authority involved. These books are essential for detailed prescribing as no homoeopath can remember the thousands of remedies contained within their pages. Computer technology has been a wonderful aid to homoeopathy, specifically with regards to the complex and time-consuming process of analyzing the symptoms of the individual patient and coming up with potentially indicated remedies, from which the homoeopath can then choose the simillimum. In first-aid homoeopathy, the simillimum is the remedy that covers the essence of the sick person as shown by the symptoms. It is often called the 'indicated remedy' and covers the illness **and** the patient's individual response to the illness.

SYMPTOMS

The remedy pictures given in the Materia Medica chapter are highly condensed summaries and include information that will be very useful to you. The remedy picture contains many kinds of symptoms but not all symptoms are of equal importance and all are valued and classified uniquely. Objective symptoms that can be observed, like a flushed, red face or a wet slimy tongue, are as important as subjective symptoms such as a weepy mood (for which *Pulsatilla* should be used) or the sensation of a bursting pain (*Belladonna* would be indicated for this).

Symptoms can be classified into the following categories:

- **Common** symptoms. These are symptoms of the diagnosis, for example a runny nose and a cold. These symptoms are also common to most illnesses and most people when they are ill, for instance tiredness. As they are not distinctive, these common symptoms are not very useful in finding the specific remedy.
- **Local** or **particular** symptoms are symptoms for which we use the word '**my**', for example 'my nose', 'my throat', 'my head'.
- **General** symptoms are symptoms of how the whole body feels or reacts. With general symptoms we will use the word '**I**' as in 'I feel chilly', 'I am thirsty', 'I am restless', 'I am weepy'. (When thinking or speaking of her child, a mother will say, 'He is irritable.' Remember that if the child could speak or explain himself, he would declare 'I am irritable'.) Food desires and cravings or aversions, as well as reactions to temperature or weather, are also considered to be general symptoms. All the symptoms of the emotions, especially those that have changed since the person has been ill, are very important general symptoms. Particular and general symptoms are, by their nature, found together in the description of an illness. Sometimes the ill person will feel very chilly (general) with a sore head (particular).
- Other important symptoms are those of **causation**. Causation refers to what may have weakened someone's immune system, allowing the underlying susceptibility to become affected. Shocks, being caught in the rain, being overtired and emotionally upset among other triggers can induce ill health. Symptoms of causation are mainly general, for example 'I became ill **after the fright**' (*Gelsemium*) or 'the child has croup **after being in the cold wind**' (*Aconite*).
- **Strange**, **rare** or **peculiar** symptoms are unusual to the sickness, to the sick person or to our common sense, for example a high fever with no thirst (*Pulsatilla*), laughing in grief (*Ignatia*), or requiring hard pressure to improve the pain of an inflamed knee (*Bryonia*). These very important symptoms are unique to the sick person and make it much easier to find the remedy.
- **Concomitant** symptoms are symptoms that occur at the same time as the main complaint but are not directly connected to it, for example fright with aching in the body (*Gelsemium*).

WHAT ARE MODALITIES?

A modality is the symptom that expresses the individuality of the sick person, for example one person's pain is better for warmth, while another's pain is worsened by warmth. The modality expands the symptom by describing it more fully. In our remedy pictures, the 'modalities' are clearly expressed as **Better/Worse facts**.

> **COMPLETE SYMPTOMS**
>
> A **complete symptom** on which we can base our choice of remedy is hard to find as it would include:
>
> **causation** – what caused the illness?
>
> **location** – where is it?
>
> **sensation** – what does it feel like?
>
> **modality** (**Better/Worse facts**) – what makes the illness, you or the pain feel better or worse?
>
> **concomitants** – what has occurred at the same time as the illness, but separate from the illness?

A complete symptom is, however, not necessary for an accurate prescription. It has been said that a three-legged stool is stable. In other words, three unequivocal symptoms will give a reliable lead to the correct remedy. The more distinctly the symptom differs from the person's normal state, the more important the symptom becomes. A sweet-natured, placid person showing intense irritability would, for example, be in great need of a remedy like *Hepar sulph*, *Chamomilla* or *Nux vom* to treat irritation.

In injury, as another example, the type of tissue involved would be very important. For instance, *Arnica* would be good for soft-tissue injury, *Rhus tox* for injury to tendons or ligaments and *Hypericum* for injury to nerves, like hurting a finger in the car's door.

In homoeopathy we accept that the symptoms are the efforts (sometimes ineffectual) of the body to heal itself. For instance, a fever is necessary to raise the level of interferon in the bloodstream to fight viral infections, and diarrhoea is often the body's response to toxic food (in these cases, diarrhoea can sometimes become excessive). Although we are working with the symptoms of the sick person, homoeopathy is not only a symptomatic treatment. It utilizes the symptom picture as a guide to how the whole individual is reacting to his complaint.

'Homoeopathy subscribes to an underlying vitalistic theory which holds that intrinsic to all vital phenomena there is a life-giving, life-preserving, life-directing and integrating force in every living organism.' (quoted from H Gaier).

This embraces the concept that the living system has an ability to maintain itself and will always attempt to heal itself. The remedies used in homoeopathy are dynamic and the living system is dynamic. Another similarity! Homoeopathy is a holistic, life-centred, vitalistic form of therapeutic medicine.

ACUTE DISEASES

In homoeopathic terms, 'acute' diseases, such as colds, food poisoning or chickenpox, are considered to be self-limiting, that is, they have a beginning or incubation stage, a middle stage of symptoms, and a convalescent phase at the end. Correct treatment with homoeopathy will alleviate the symptoms, reduce the length of the illness and speed up recovery. It can also prevent secondary infections and complications from developing.

There are many different types of acute disease

- Injuries, for example sprains, strains, burns, food poisoning, and so on. In this category, we need to deal with the injury to the body and any emotional trauma that resulted from the injury.
- Fixed acute diseases with a definite pattern, such as chickenpox. Remedies definitely make the disease a 'non-event' with no secondary complications.
- Coughs, colds and other viral infections. These depend on the person being susceptible and able to 'catch' the disease.
- Flare-ups of a chronic condition, for example recurrent attacks of sinusitis. In this condition the sick person's susceptibility is constantly being triggered and manifests as acute flare-ups of the chronic underlying condition. Another way of putting it would be that the chronic disease of sinusitis is a continuous underlying illness in the sick person. He is not aware of it when well and yet with his individual specific triggers, for example pollution, change of weather, excess cheese, and so on, he will manifest an acute episode of sinusitis. These recurrent, acute attacks of sinusitis show up a chronic underlying tendency or illness.

CHRONIC DISEASES

A chronic disease is much more deep-seated than an acute disease. It develops slowly and unpredictably and sick people are not able to eradicate it by themselves. We could say that the sick person's susceptibility to 'that illness' is very strong. Examples are recurrent boils, styes, depression, asthma, eczema, irritable bowel syndrome, and so on. The treatment of the acute flare-up of these chronic problems will alleviate each attack, but not cure the underlying condition.

The treatment of chronic disease is one of the strong points of homoeopathy. By treating at a deeper level, the sick person's system can be helped either to eradicate the illness or minimize it. The result will be no further acute attacks or fewer attacks that are far milder. This will depend on the curability and genetic background, lifestyle and degree of suppressive treatment that has preceded chronic deep 'constitutional' treatment. Remember that this constitutional treatment should only be undertaken by a professional homoeopath, as it takes many years of training to acquire this kind of skill and knowledge.

In the home situation, the 'acute' or everyday illness can be treated easily and safely. However, it is important to recognize when a recurrent acute illness is part of a deeper chronic problem and requires further professional help. A telltale sign of this is when the acute conditions tend to become recurrent. For example, tonsillitis may recur frequently despite treatment and good lifestyle management such as the elimination of junk food from the diet, and so on. A person suffering from this would require deeper constitutional homoeopathy to deal with the total susceptibility of his whole body to continually come down with bouts of tonsillitis.

SUPPRESSION

For your interest, we will mention some philosophical issues dealt with in the treatment of chronic disease that are not really relevant to the treatment of acute illnesses as discussed in this book.

Constantine Hering (1800–1880), who took homoeopathy to America, was responsible for many provings, notably that of the snake remedy *Lachesis*. He established the first homoeopathic medical school in Pennsylvania and wrote many books on homoeopathy. He remarked that cure had a tendency to occur in a definite pattern. It would appear that the path one walked along in the journey to ill health needs to be retraced on the journey to cure and good health. This means that illnesses of the past may return in a pale, shadowy, transitory manner, often in the reverse order of their original appearance.

Another observation is that cure occurs in a particular direction. This is 'from above down' and 'from within out'. For example, a person suffering from asthma may experience hay fever and then eczema while in the healing process. The eczema will often clear away from the head first and the hands and feet last.

By thinking about these observations the concept of suppression of symptoms becomes clearer. Suppression can take place when only single symptoms rather than the whole person are treated. A common example of a chronic disease would be eczema. If the eczema alone is treated with cortisone or any other therapy that concentrates on the skin only, the process that induces the eczema will have a tendency to continue recurring and often appear to spread. If suppressive treatment is continued and the eczema finally clears up, the eczema illness will go underground and can manifest in later years as asthma. In an attempt to cure the sick person using the homoeopathic method, the whole person and her asthma, plus her past history of eczema, will be taken into consideration. The alleviation of the asthma will often be accompanied by a return of the original 'eczema illness' that then in turn needs to be cleared.

Another commonly experienced form of suppression from the homoeopathic standpoint would be the removal of warts by whatever method without taking into consideration the whole person who has them. When the warts (the single symptom) are burnt off or painted away, the disturbed vital force of the person that produced these warts will be forced into making many more warts or it will go into a more internal or aggressive mode. This could be compared to pruning a tree – the effect will in fact be to stimulate more growth.

MIASMS

Another fascinating philosophical concept in homoeopathy is the theory of miasms. A miasm is a mode in which the body reacts. Homoeopathy postulates that the body can respond in three major ways. **These are:**

- underactivity
- excess activity
- degenerative activity.

An example of underactivity or hypofunction would be the inability to assimilate food or iron, resulting in allergies, chronic anaemia or failure to thrive. Groundless anxiety is an emotional expression of this reactive mode.

Hyperfunction can be well illustrated by the body's tendency to overproduce mucus, catarrh, warts, and so on. In the emotional sphere there may be excessive-compulsive behaviour or hyperactivity. The degenerative phase is illustrated in the tendency to destructive behaviour, such as suicidal depression and schizophrenia, or on a physical level with diseases such as multiple sclerosis and cancer.

Genetic or inherited illness tendencies are also covered by the miasmatic theory and a professional homoeopath will want to know about the patterns of illness in the extended family background. This is a very brief summary of a very complex subject in homoeopathy. The aim of chronic treatment is to help the sick person stay on the road to health. Health is a process, not an absolute, of freedom from discomfort or pain. Conversely, disease is a limitation of freedom.

CONSTITUTIONAL TYPES

In *The Science of Homoeopathy,* George Vithoulkas defines a person's constitution as 'the genetic inheritance tempered or modified by the environment'. He is in fact stating that a person's state of health (or disease), combined with the temperament or the way he will react emotionally or physically in a particular environment or circumstance, will produce a constitutional type. This constitutional type must be matched with a remedy capable of producing a similar pattern. This remedy is called the constitutional remedy for that particular individual at that particular time, and will be necessary in the treatment of chronic conditions.

To expand on this idea, we all have a basic individualized personality, emotional and genetic history, strongly marked reactions to weather, food likes and dislikes, menstrual history, when applicable, sleep and dream patterns, our past history of illnesses, and specific reactive modes (miasms). This assessment would produce a baseline of susceptibility that can be modified by the use of a constitutional remedy.

State of health + genetic make-up + physical/emotional response + disease process + miasmatic background + past illness = constitution at this particular time.

TOTALITY OF SYMPTOMS

In times of illness, we often say 'we are not ourselves'. This ill or 'not ourself' part demonstrates changes when we are ill. It represents a shift from our own baseline. This change in ourselves, coupled with the illness we are suffering plus our very 'individual' reaction to the illness, forms a totality of symptoms.

Sometimes when we become ill we become 'too much of ourselves'. For example, an irritable person becomes aggressive and angry. Occasionally the constitutional prescription remains the basic personality type albeit in an exaggerated form.

Of course our very basic physical build, for instance bone size, height, colouring, and so on, remains unchanged. However, weight changes and wear and tear do occur and might be of consideration in this totality. One hears people in the homoeopathic world speaking of '*Calc carb* types' or '*Phosphorus* types'. These types must be seen as very generalized aspects of the remedy or personality, which are only sometimes of use in an illness or in treating the whole person with a deep-acting constitutional remedy. You may read in some books that the '*Pulsatilla* type' is blonde and blue-eyed. This is quite ridiculous in the multicultural world in which we live. A remedy will work if it matches the symptom picture and modalities of the ill person irrespective of colour or creed.

> *'Mental and emotional diseases are not sharply separated from other classes of disease, because in every disease the mental and emotional state is altered.'*
>
> SAMUEL HAHNEMANN

MISCONCEPTIONS

Let us discuss the many misconceptions that surround homoeopathy. For completeness, let us list what homoeopathy is **not**.

Homoeopathy is NOT herbalism: Herbs are **not** chosen based on the Law of Similars and have a chemical pharmacological action even though they are in their natural state. If a herb were to be selected on the basis of similarity, it would become possible for it to be a homoeopathic prescription.

Homoeopathy is NOT naturopathy: Naturopathy uses the diet as medicine, combined with natural treatments such as water therapies, compresses, sweating, lifestyle changes, and so on. Homoeopaths do give dietary advice as an adjunct. Hahnemann in *The Organon* insists upon 'removing all obstacles to cure'. A diet full of junk food is **not** conducive to healing, neither is a lifestyle in which you watch scary movies on TV conducive to restful sleep.

Homoeopathy is NOT vitamins: Vitamins may be useful or necessary additions. For example, iron-deficient anaemia may be due to a lack of iron in the diet, which must be supplemented, and/or a lack of absorption of the iron, which will require the correct remedy chosen according to homoeopathic principles.

Homoeopathy is NOT chiropractic, osteopathic or physiotherapy treatment: These treatments are often necessary and malpositions of the body can be 'obstacles to cure'.

Homoeopathy is NOT the use of pendulums or radionics: Some homoeopathic practitioners are known to use these techniques in their practices as an aid.

Homoeopathy is NOT witchcraft, cult or religion: You do **not** have to 'believe' in order for a correct homoeopathic prescription to work.

Homoeopathy is NOT a placebo: Outstanding results can be achieved on domestic animals, large herds of cattle, unconscious patients and, of course, babies and children.

Homoeopathy is NOT against operations, tests or medical diagnoses: Tests and medical diagnoses are of great assistance in identifying a disease and enabling you to make a more accurate prognosis of its course and eventual outcome. There are many conditions nowadays for which it is almost impossible to confirm the clinical diagnosis, but by applying homoeopathy, these conditions can be treated successfully. We have different parameters and capabilities in treatment and prognosis.

Homoeopathy is NOT acupuncture, acupressure or traditional Chinese medicine: A completely different rationale is applied in the use of and treatment by these disciplines.

Homoeopathy is NOT the use of 'a purported homoeopathic remedy on the shelf': The correct selection according to the Law of Similars makes the remedy homoeopathic. (The quote is from personal communication with Dr. R. Linder.)

Homoeopathy is NOT a system that does not require knowledge of pathology, physiology, anatomy, examination, use of laboratory tests, and so on: It is imperative for the homoeopath to understand the norms of illness in order to be able to determine whether something deviates from the 'well baseline', to determine a prognosis and to assess the efficacy of the treatment. One of the advantages of homoeopathy is the fact that you can still prescribe for a sick person who does not have a 'diagnostic label' as you will prescribe on the symptom picture presented.

Homoeopathy is NOT harmless: It is definitely non-toxic and non-iatrogenic, that is it does not cause new illnesses or accumulate in the body causing toxic reactions. If you stay within the limits of this book and do not enter into deeper constitutional treatment, there can be no dangerous effects. However, for any treatment to effect a change in an ilness, it must have potential power and should therefore be used respectfully.

Homoeopathy is NOT disrespectful to other therapies: It is not always advantageous to combine a number of different therapies even though they may each be effective and highly respected disciplines. The symptom picture may be obscured, making accurate prescribing difficult. When in doubt, consult your homoeopath.

Homoeopathy is NOT outdated and anti-research: Even a cursory search on the Internet will provide many research articles and projects that have been and are currently being undertaken. Many new and fascinating remedies are being proved and their pictures published.

PART TWO

MATERIA MEDICA

ACONITUM *(Aconite napellus)*
Monkshood

Source facts
Tincture of whole poisonous plant and root when beginning to flower.

Chat facts
This deadly poison has been converted by the homoeopathic method of dilution and potentization into a totally safe medicine suitable even for newborn babies if indicated.

> **Key facts**
> - To be used at the very beginning or **early** in the symptoms
> - Conditions caused by or accompanied by **shock** and fright
> - Complaints caused by exposure to **dry, cold winds** or sudden changes of temperature
> - Conditions rapidly becoming very acute
> - Restlessness

Description facts
- The sick person suffers high anxiety, is very fearful (even of imminent death) or cannot recover from shock or fright. This is the first remedy to think of after being hijacked, mugged or abused.
- The pains of *Aconite*, that is the pains that would cause you to think that *Aconite* is the matching remedy (the simillimum), are usually intense, intolerable, sometimes with pins and needles or tingling, and are often accompanied by great restlessness. The sick person may be sleepless from nightmares or anxious dreams.
- Cold, dry weather can bring on sudden, severe croup with a hoarse, dry, hacking cough, often starting at night or around midnight, often after a warm, sunny day. The child grasps his throat with every cough. When comfortably warm, the shock of sudden cold weather, the draught from a very cold air conditioner or even a glass of ice-cold water can also trigger inflammation and fevers. Remember that not all of these symptoms have to show in any one sick person or condition, thus the mental restlessness or anxiety may or may not be present.

- One cheek may be red and the other pale (compare *Chamomilla*, page 60, *Ipecac*, page 75, and *Pulsatilla*, page 93) and the ears are hot and red.
- The nose is blocked and dry or it can present in the form of a watery cold with a hot discharge. This cold begins suddenly.
- Sudden bleeding, for example from the nose, can occur. The blood will be bright red and will be accompanied by great anxiety and fear. It can be caused by a fright.
- The person needing *Aconite* has a thirst for cold water.
- Children can experience watery diarrhoea on hot days or from drinking ice cold drinks when very hot.

Better/worse facts	
Better:	**Worse:**
Open air	Dry, cold winds
Sweating	Getting chilled
Rest	Night, especially midnight
	Warmth
	Violent emotions

User-friendly facts
Remember *Aconite* even for the long-distant effects of fright, for the person who has not been well since a bad shock as long as 25 years ago. Fear and anxiety will make the sick person feel that he is sicker than he really is, and could even die. All the senses are highly sensitive to noise and pain. Think of this remedy after severe injuries or operations.

Clinical facts
Anxiety, croup, common cold, cough, earache, eye injuries, fever, insomnia, laryngitis, shock from injury, surgery.

Danger facts
See **Fever, Danger facts**, page 162
Croup *see* **Cough, Danger facts**, page 137

ALLIUM CEPA (*Allium cepa*)
Red onion

Source facts

Potentized tincture of the whole fresh plant.

Chat facts

Earlier we described the reaction to onion, *Allium cepa*, to explain the homoeopathic principle of similarity of the remedy to the sick person's disease symptoms. However, the question we now need to ask is: 'What is the action of *Allium cepa* that individualizes it so that we can use it accurately?'

> **Key facts**
> - Increased discharge from nose, eyes and larynx
> - **Colds** and **hay fever**
> - **Acrid nasal** discharges with sneezing
> - Burning, smarting or **bland, watering eyes** (lacrimation)
> - Sensitivity to light (photophobia)
> - Colds from damp, cold weather
> - Hacking cough from breathing in cold air

Description facts

- The hay fever of *Allium cepa* has lots of sneezing with a burning, watery discharge from the nose. The symptoms can be caused by the smell or pollen of flowers or from eating fuzzy peaches. When the sick person enters a warm room the sneezing is worse and is often accompanied by hoarseness and tickling in the larynx (voice box).
- The colds of *Allium cepa* are very similar to hay fever and may be one-sided (occurring in one nostril). The nasal discharge burns so much and is so acrid that it irritates the nostrils and upper lip. The eyes are red and burning, but the tears are bland. There is tickling in the larynx or a hoarse, dry, painful cough. The cough feels better in a warm room, but the cold is worse in a warm room and feels better for cool air. There can be a hacking cough from inspiring cold air.

Better/worse facts	
Better:	**Worse:**
Colds better for fresh air	Cough is worse from cold air
	Cold is worse in a warm room

User-friendly facts
Allium cepa is a simple but effective remedy for a specific type of common cold and a specific type of hay fever.

Clinical facts
Colds, eye infections (conjunctivitis), hay fever, laryngitis.

Danger facts
Nothing significant.

APIS MELLIFICA (*Apis*)
Honey bee

Source facts
A tincture made from the whole bee, which is then potentized.

Chat facts
A bee sting causes redness, burning, swelling and stinging. As you already know from the Law of Similars, *Apis* will cure ailments that have redness, burning, swelling and stinging.

> **Key facts**
> - Excessive watery **swelling**, often pink-red and often in the throat or on the skin
> - Urticaria (also known as hives or allergic skin reaction) with oedema, swelling and intolerable **itching** weals
> - Swelling of joints

> **Key facts – continued**
> - Pains are burning, darting, stinging; better for cold applications (opposite to *Ars alb*, page 49)
> - Anxious restlessness
> - Clumsy, drops things easily
> - No thirst
> - Worse for all forms of heat
> - Great sensitivity to touch

Description facts

- This remedy is almost self-explanatory as most of us have witnessed or experienced the effects of a bee sting. The allergic reactions with their severe swellings and oedema can range from urticaria to bags of water under and on the eyes to a closing up of the throat. The urticaria has intolerable itching. The swelling can also be inside a joint.
- Eye inflammation (conjunctivitis) is accompanied by intense sensitivity to light, hot tears and puffy, swollen eyelids.
- The inflamed throat with swollen sack-like uvula (little tongue) has a stinging fishbone sensation and is better for cold drinks. The tonsils are swollen and fiery red with stinging pain.
- Children fuss and whine, fidget and weep (compare *Pulsatilla*, page 93).

Better/worse facts	
Better:	Worse:
Cold air, bathing, drinks and applications	Heated room, fire, drinks
Uncovering herself	Warm bed
Sitting erect	Slight touch and pressure

User-friendly facts

Pinky-red colour and swelling accompanied by stinging pain will lead you to think of *Apis* wherever it may be showing. Similarly *Apis* conditions will never tolerate warmth.

Clinical facts
Allergy, burns, hay fever, insect bites, measles, sore throats, styes, sunburn, urticaria.

Danger facts
Angio-neurotic oedema (an acute allergic episode of swelling of the internal organs such as the throat and windpipe) with inability to breathe. Seek immediate help.

ARNICA (*Arnica montana*)
Bruisewort, Leopardbane

Source facts
Potentized tincture of whole fresh plant including the root.

Chat facts
This herb grows on high mountains and is renowned among mountaineers for preventing altitude sickness and treating the effects of overexertion. Its outstanding effect on all injuries and traumas has made *Arnica* a household name. The cream or tincture should not be used externally on broken skin as it can cause irritation. In this case, rather consider *Calendula* (*see* page 55). The potency should, however, be taken orally to reduce the effects of injuries both physically and emotionally.

Key facts
- **Trauma**, physical and mental
- Effects of trauma, immediate or long term
- 'Leave me alone, there is nothing wrong with me'
- **Shock**, mental and physical
- **Injuries**, **falls**, sprains, blows, **bruises**, fractures
- Black eye (*see also* Symphytum, page 105)
- Sore, bruised sensation
- **Altitude** sickness
- Flu with sore, bruised muscles
- Septic conditions like small boils in recurrent attacks

> **Key facts – continued**
> - Effects of excessive heat
> - Effects of **overexertion**, overwork, fatigue with aching
> - Waking at night with fear after an accident

Description facts

- After an accident, however major or minor, you must think of *Arnica* first. Often the injured person will tell you that there is nothing the matter with her and will refuse medical assistance or even simple care. Even at roadside accidents an obviously injured person will tell you that 'she is fine' but she will wake at night in emotional shock, aching, feeling weak and will complain that the bed is too hard.
- *Arnica* is the first remedy to be thought of for any bruising as it aids the body in absorbing the effects of tissue bleeding. It also helps the body to absorb lactic acid and can thus be used after too much exercise to prevent muscle stiffness the next day (*Rhus tox*, *see* page 96). The word 'excess' in many ways describes some *Arnica* conditions, for example excess heat, excess altitude, excess physical work, excess mental work, excess shock, excess stress, excess aching, excess injury with bleeding or bruising.
- When a person is in shock and needs *Arnica*, her body produces foul-smelling odours. The mouth can smell like rotten eggs after dental work.

Better/worse facts	
Better:	Worse:
Lying with head low and body stretched out	Injury
Rest	Overexertion
	Touch, being approached when in shock

User-friendly facts

This is probably the one remedy known by most people for its wonderful and helpful effects in all cases where the body's equilibrium has been disturbed by injury or overstrains of all types. Remember to use *Arnica* postoperatively and after childbirth.

Clinical facts
Bruising, black eye, boils, childbirth, exhaustion, fractures, injuries, overexertion, post-surgery, shock, sprains.

Danger facts
It has become common to use *Arnica* for weeks to prepare for surgery or labour. This shows a misunderstanding of the homoeopathic principles and can sometimes *lead* to bleeding instead of *preventing* it. If you administer a remedy repeatedly for a long period of time when there is no similarity to the sickness, that is you are administering it to a healthy person, it is possible to produce a 'proving'. Remember that *Arnica* can cause bleeding in the proving and therefore cure bleeding **if there are *Arnica* symptoms**. Therefore it is perfectly safe to use just after trauma or surgery. However, people taking blood-thinning medication should avoid taking *Arnica* as it can interact and increase the chances of bleeding.

ARSENICUM ALBUM (*Ars alb*)
Arsenious acid

Source facts
A trituration, dilution and potentization of the substance.

Chat facts
The medicine, when potentized, is gentle enough to be used on a newborn baby, yet is highly effective whenever it is indicated for any age.

> **Key facts**
> - **Anxiety** and fear
> - **Restlessness**
> - Great **weakness** and exhaustion, often from minor causes
> - Ailments worse between **midnight and 3 a.m.**
> - **Burning** pains which are better for warmth
> - **Chilliness**

> **Key facts – continued**
> - Vomiting at the same time as having diarrhoea
> - Desire for orderliness and tidiness when ill
> - Fear of being alone

Description facts

- The sick person feels cold and is unable to warm up. He takes hot baths, sits near the heater and feels really weak and washed out. The cold begins – the eyes run, the nose runs, all the watery discharge burns and even a tissue to the nose hurts. In spite of all the burning only warmth is welcome and he lies all bundled up, needing a little fresh air in the room (in this detail it is quite opposite to *Hepar sulph*, see page 69). He is frequently thirsty for sips of water or warm drinks.
- There may be a dry, tight feeling in the chest and a dry, tight cough that makes the sick person unable to rest in one place. So he gets up and lies on the couch for a while and then tiredly moves back to bed.
- A small child will restlessly change from one person to another while being carried. He dislikes being left alone and his anxiety and fears increase after midnight. He becomes fussily tidy and wants things lined up very neatly.
- *Ars alb* is the most important food poisoning remedy. An *Ars alb* patient gets sick from bad meats, poultry, eggs, melons or ice cream. His reaction to the food poisoning is more important than whatever made him ill. He tends to wake up from midnight until 3 a.m. feeling an intense nausea. There is often diarrhoea and vomiting, accompanied by great weakness as if he is going to faint. There may be nausea or retching after seeing or taking in any food or drink. The diarrhoea can be offensive and burning. Weakness, prostration and restlessness are commonly present too.

Better/worse facts	
Better:	**Worse:**
Heat	Cold (likes cold compresses to the head)
Motion, moving about restlessly	Contaminated food
Company	Midnight to 3 a.m.
	Being alone

User-friendly facts
The chief signs that point you to *Ars alb* often lie in the whole picture, which is one of weakness out of proportion to the complaint, great anxiety and even fear of death (*Aconite*, *see* page 42), a fear of being alone and restlessness.

Clinical facts
Allergies, anxiety, asthma, colds, coughs, diarrhoea, extreme weakness with fevers and flu, food poisoning, hay fever, headaches, vomiting.

Danger facts
Dehydration from excessive loss of fluid and vomiting. The skin loses its elasticity and doesn't go down again when pinched. No urine is passed. The mouth is dry.
Asthma or tight chest that does not respond promptly.

BELLADONNA (*Atropa belladonna*)
Deadly Nightshade, Witch's Berry

Source facts
Made from the tincture of the whole poisonous plant when beginning to flower.

Chat facts
Again the dilution and potentization process renders this poisonous plant wonderfully effective and totally safe. The name Belladonna means 'beautiful lady' and derives from a custom Italian ladies practiced to drop the juice of this plant into their eyes to dilate their pupils. However, with their dilated pupils, they could not see their intended!

> **Key facts**
> - Early stages of **inflammation**
> - **Sudden** onset of symptoms, quickly becoming severe
> - **Red**, flushed face
> - Hot, dry, red skin and mucous membranes

> **Key facts – continued**
> - **Throbbing**, pulsating conditions, e.g. headaches and boils, strong palpitations
> - High **fevers**, even delirium with intense heat
> - Shiny eyes with dilated pupils, sensitivity to light (photophobia)
> - Hot head with cold limbs
> - Hypersensitive to being jarred, touch, pressure, light
> - **Burning**, **Inflammations**, **Red**, **Dry** and **Sudden** (use the acronym BIRDS to remember this)
> - Effects of sunstroke
> - Bleeding – blood is bright red, hot and gushing
> - Sudden, violent colic
> - Ailments are frequently on the right side of the body

Description facts

The *Belladonna* picture is best described as follows:

- The well child suddenly becomes ill at 3 p.m. Within an hour he has a dry, hot fever, flushed red face, mottled red skin and tongue resembling a strawberry. His eyes are bright and shiny with large, dilated pupils. He may have a little dry, hard or barking cough. On opening his mouth you will see a bright red throat or tonsils that look like cherry tomatoes. His throat feels dry. It is hard to confine this child to bed because he grows wilder as his fever increases. His feet are cold and his body feels steaming hot under the covers. Soon he has an earache and will not tolerate any touch. Before there are any complications or delirium, *Belladonna* is indicated and is capable of halting the illness.
- Consider *Belladonna* for that throbbing, red, hypersensitive boil before pus formation, often red-streaked, or that violent, pulsating headache, or symptoms from overexposure to the sun.
- Remember this remedy for acute colic – in this case the sick person will hate any jarring of the bed or the jarring of walking. The pains are worse by pressure.
- The bleeding of *Belladonna* is bright red, hot and gushing, and often accompanied by a red face, for instance in a nosebleed.
- People needing *Belladonna* often have restless sleep, may jerk in their sleep, grind their teeth and have unpleasant nightmares.

Better/worse facts	
Better:	**Worse:**
Sitting upright, bending backwards	Lying down
	At 3 p.m.
	Heat of sun
	Washing or cutting hair
	Jarring, motion
	Touch
	Noise

User-friendly facts
The sudden and rather acute onset of a headache or fever, sore throat, and so on, with its throbbing, hot nature, will direct you to *Belladonna*.

Clinical facts
Bleeding, colic, headaches, high fever, inflammations, for example boils, laryngitis, fiery red skin rashes, sore ears and sore throats, sunstroke.

Danger facts
Fever *see* **Fever, Danger facts**, page 162

BRYONIA (*Bryonia alba*)
Wild hops, White bryony

Source facts
Tincture of root harvested before flowering.

Chat facts
A wild, climbing hedgerow plant that has been used as a herb for thousands of years despite its toxicity. It grows slowly – and the onset of symptoms is slow.

> **Key facts**
> - **Worse for any motion**, for example breathing, moving eyes, coughing, and so on
> - Better from **pressure**
> - **Stitching**, tearing pains, worse for motion, better for rest
> - **Dryness** of mucous membranes, mouth, lips and throat, and white-coated tongue
> - Swelling and inflammation of membranes lining joints
> - Intense **irritability**
> - Desire to be left alone, quietly
> - Desire to go home
> - **Thirst for large quantities** of liquid
> - Dry, hacking cough
> - Slow onset of illness
> - Headache
> - Vertigo, dizzy or faint on rising

Description facts

- The *Bryonia* patient has been feeling off-colour for many days. He longs to be at home, cozily tucked up in a warm bed. The slightest movement worsens his bursting headache. It helps a little to press onto the pain or to lie on his sore side – in fact, it is best not to move at all as even blinking his eyes seems to make it worse. He aches and as he turns in the bed, the stitching pains go through his painful rheumatic knee-joint. He wishes he had a tight bandage to put on his sore joint. His irritability when disturbed is matched by his irritability on moving.
- He drinks his glass of water in one go and is thirsty for another, but is irritated by the effort of asking for more. He worries and frets about being absent from his work. He even dreamt of being at work all night long.
- If a dry, hard cough begins, the person needing *Bryonia* will hold his chest to stop the stitching, tearing pain behind the breastbone as he coughs. (In the case of a headache, a *Bryonia* patient would hold his head.)
- When the sick person tries to get out of bed to urinate, he feels almost faint with dizziness and wishes he never had to move again.

Better/worse facts	
Better:	**Worse:**
Rest	Movement
Pressure	Disturbance
Drinking large quantities of liquid	At 9 p.m.
Warmth	

User-friendly facts

In *Bryonia* the modality of being **aggravated by any motion** is a keynote of all physical or mental ailments. *Bryonia* patients are irritated by being disturbed or even having to answer questions. They just want to go home and be left alone. Even children prefer not to be carried about and want to lie still in their beds.

Remember *Bryonia* for fractures, sprains and torn ligaments that are very painful and have the *Bryonia* modalities.

Clinical facts

Cough, flu, headache, migraines, rheumatism, vertigo.

Danger facts

Nothing significant.

CALENDULA (*Calendula officinalis*)
Marigold

Source facts

Tincture of whole plant, especially flowers. Both the tincture and the potentized tincture can be used in many ways.

Chat facts

Calendula can be used to prevent infections. It is very effective in the treatment of wounds, promoting the growth of tissue, which helps close and heal wounds. Because of its tannin content it will stop bleeding and is best applied with firm pressure.

> **Key facts**
> - Stops bleeding
> - Prevents suppuration and infection
> - **Promotes healing** of open wounds and ulcers
> - Takes pain out of injuries, tears, cuts and grazes

Description facts

- Make a warm solution of the tincture and apply *Calendula* as a compress to reduce pain in open injuries. (Remember *Arnica* may not be applied to open wounds.) While using it externally, a potency of *Calendula* 6ch should be taken internally.
- For nosebleeds, soak a ball of cotton wool in the tincture and insert into the bleeding nostril (*see* Bleeding, page 118).
- Use 15 drops of *Calendula* tincture in a little warm water as a gargle for sore throats, after tooth extractions or dental work and gum surgery. It will aid healing and stop bleeding. Many gynaecologists frequently use *Calendula* to help heal tissue damage after childbirth.
- The cream is soothing and healing, gentle enough for nappy rashes too.

> **Better/worse facts**
>
> These are not especially differentiating in this remedy

User-friendly facts

Keep this handy remedy in the bathroom, kitchen and with your remedy kit, in potency, tincture and cream form wherever you may travel.

Clinical facts

Abrasions, burns, after childbirth, for torn, injured or broken wounds.

Danger facts

See **Bleeding, Danger facts**, page 118
See **Injury, Danger signs**, page 177

CANTHARIS (*Cantharis vesicatoria*)
Spanish fly

Source facts
Potentized tincture of whole Spanish fly.

Chat facts
Despite its source, once this remedy has been potentized it becomes a wonderfully safe, effective and rapidly acting remedy to be used when indicated by the symptom picture.

> **Key facts**
> - **Cystitis** (inflammation of the bladder)
> - Violent, sudden onset
> - Pain is **burning**, cutting and **severe** and accompanies urination
> - Severe burning, and continued desire to urinate after urination
> - Skin complaints with large **water blisters**
> - Skin reactions to **burns** and sunburn

Description facts
- Think of this remedy when there is burning or for the effects of burns. The pain is always intense. The burns feel better from cold applications. The skin tends to form vesicles or large watery blisters. **Do not** pop these blisters as the underlying raw skin would be prone to infections.
- This is the first remedy to think of when there is an attack of cutting, smarting, burning pain on passing urine (also consider *Merc sol*, page 82).

Better/worse facts	
Better:	**Worse:**
Warmth	Passing urine
Rubbing	

User-friendly facts

This little remedy may be a useful addition to your kit. It works effectively in a 6ch potency.

Clinical facts

Burns, cystitis, sunburn.

Danger facts

Cystitis (bladder infection) – if burning on passing urine does not subside within 24 hours, or if there is a high fever or blood in the urine, seek professional help.
See **Burns, Danger facts**, page 124

CARBO VEG (*Carbo vegetabilis*)
Vegetable charcoal

Source facts

Wood charcoal made from the finest beech wood stripped of its bark, triturated and potentized.

Chat facts

Crude charcoal (not potentized) has been used in folk medicine as a deodorant, disinfectant and antiseptic. In present times it is used for digestive discomforts like flatulence.

Key facts

- **Collapses** with desire to be fanned (corpse reviver – *see* opposite)
- Extreme **exhaustion** from present or previous illness (has not been well since)
- Physical shock leading to collapse
- Effects of loss of fluids (diarrhoea, vomiting)
- **Needs air** – must be fanned or have windows open
- Faints easily
- Burning pains

> **Key facts – continued**
> - Sensitive to cold, cold to touch with internal heat
> - Bad effects of rich food, **bad fish** or meat, alcohol, carbon monoxide poisoning, ice water
> - Flatulence and belching
> - Distended, painful abdomen

Description facts

- The collapse can be brought on from long, exhausting illnesses, loss of fluids, excessive bleeding, after surgical operations and severe food poisonings. The keynote of *Carbo veg* is always the desire for air, whether by fanning or a desire to sit in front of open windows. The sick person is ice cold to the touch and sometimes looks bluish yet feels hot internally. This remedy brings about such quick relief to a very ill and collapsed person that it has become known as the 'corpse reviver' (it is imperative that you seek professional help while treating him).
- He struggles with digestion but the air problem is internal. *Carbo veg* is known for its vast production and accumulation of air/gas – 'the winds'! The *Carbo veg* patient either struggles to pass the accumulation of air or battles to stop it passing. The odorous, offensive wind or gases are burped out upwards and passed downwards. He can often experience wind-colic and can't tolerate anything tight around the distended middle.

Better/worse facts	
Better:	Worse:
Cool air	Warmth
Fanning	Loss of fluid
Belching	Exhausting diseases
Elevating the feet	Rich food
	Pressure of clothes

User-friendly facts

The desire for air and the production of internal gases are keynotes of *Carbo veg*.

Clinical facts
Abdominal distension and discomfort, belching, fainting, flatulent colic, flatus, lack of reaction, nosebleeds, shock.

Danger facts
Shock followed by collapse. Begin treatment immediately while getting professional help. Even if the sick person improves, a professional assessment is still required.

CHAMOMILLA (*Matricaria chamomilla*)
German chamomile

Source facts
Tincture of the whole fresh plant.

Chat facts
The uses of chamomile tea are well known – it can soothe ragged nerves, calm an irritable child and help you to sleep. This is indicative of the effects of *Chamomilla* when given in potency.

> **Key facts**
> - Bad temper, **irritability**, tantrums
> - Effects of anger
> - Oversensitivity to touch, pain, to being spoken to or looked at
> - Pains seem **unbearable**
> - Wants instant attention and relief of pain
> - One cheek may be hot and red, the other one pale and cold
> - **Desire to be carried and rocked**
> - Numbness accompanied by pain
> - **Teething**
> - Abdominal, flatulent **colic**

Description facts

- The darling *Chamomilla* child (even his mother finds that her beloved angel has become somewhat unendurable) is in an irritable, discontented mood. Nothing pleases him, nothing helps. He wants to be picked up, and when lifted up, he wants to be walked and when the walking stops, he demands his favourite toy, which he flings out of the window. At this point he proceeds to throw a tantrum. His one cheek is hot and red and his mother hopes that he is not developing an ear infection again while teething. She notices that his head is hot and sweaty, and he has green diarrhoea that looks like chopped spinach and smells like rotten eggs. When he eventually falls asleep, his eyes remain half open and he moans in his sleep.
- His mother is exhausted and grows increasingly irritable and rude. Her menstrual period is a week early from all the aggravation caused by her irrational, teething baby. She swallows painkillers for instant relief but they make her sleepy and she drinks coffee to wake herself up. She can't remember when last she had such severe cramps and her life feels like more than she can bear. It feels as if all her feathers have been ruffled. She too needs a dose of *Chamomilla* to restore her calm.

Better/worse facts	
Better:	**Worse:**
Being carried, rocked	Coffee
Walking	Analgesics
Cold applications	Alcohol
	Teething
	Anger
	Touch
	Warmth

User-friendly facts

The intense irritability, cramping pains and desire to move or be moved are marked in *Chamomilla*. The whole nervous system is hypersensitive and this is illustrated by intolerance to pain as well as quick and excessive overreaction of the emotions. There is an emotional or physical overreaction to touch. **The sick person stamps his feet and says, 'do something quickly'.**

Clinical facts
Abdominal colic, diarrhoea and ear infections, fever, painful menstruation, problems arising from excess anger, sensitivity to drugs, analgesics and coffee, teething, teething accompanied by pain, toothache.

Danger facts
Nothing significant.

COLOCYNTHIS (*Colocynthis citrillus*)
Bitter apple, Bitter cucumber

Source facts
A potentized tincture of the fruit pulp.

Chat facts
This herb was made into a purgative in Turkish folk medicine.

> **Key facts**
> - **Cramping**, twisting, grinding pains, often in the abdomen
> - Pains usually very severe
> - Sudden onset of pains, pains come in waves
> - Neuralgic pains
> - Pain is better when bending over
> - Pain much **better for hard pressure**
> - Pains may be accompanied by nausea, vomiting and urination
> - The ill effects of **anger**, indignation, inflammation
> - **Colic** and painful periods

Description facts
- The newborn baby cried inconsolably as her anxious parents paced up and down the room with her. 'I think she gets some relief,' said her father, 'when I hold her firmly against my shoulder. Maybe we should let her sleep on her tummy.' When

he put her down, the baby screamed, went red in her face and pulled up her legs. She was certainly very irritable. A dose of *Colocynthis* restored the calm.
- It is one of the most useful remedies for severe cramping anywhere in the body, but it is essential that the modalities (Better/worse facts) agree. In *Colocynthis* these modalities are very clear to see. The cramp is relieved by very hard pressure, even of a fist pressed hard into the pain, doubling up, or raising or bending the leg up onto the stomach. It is also better from the warmth of a hot pad. The sick person is restless and irritable from the pain.
- The complaints of *Colocynthis*, that is what *Colocynthis* can cause and thus cure, can be brought on by anger, indignation or by being humiliated.
- Sciatic pain in the lower back and leg is improved by pressure.

Better/worse facts	
Better:	Worse:
Warmth	Anger, indignation and humiliation
Hard pressure	
Doubling up	
Bending the leg up towards abdomen	
Movement	
Lying on the abdomen	

User-friendly facts
Abdominal colic after eating indiscretions or after gastric flu, and painful periods respond well to *Colocynthis* if it is indicated.

Clinical facts
Abdominal colic, cramps, painful periods, neuralgia (nerve pain), sciatica.

Danger facts
If acute abdominal pain persists together with hardness of the abdomen, black and very tarry stools and any bleeding in the vomit or stool, seek professional help.
See **Cramps and Colic, Danger facts**, page 142

EUPHRASIA (*Euphrasia officinalis*)
Eyebright

Source facts
Potentized tincture of the whole plant.

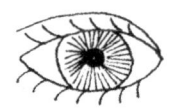

Chat facts
The name *Euphrasia* is derived from one of the classical Greek Graces and means 'gladness' as it has the properties to preserve eyesight. This herb has been used since early times for the treatment of all eye diseases.

> **Key facts**
> - **Burning, acrid, watery** discharge from **eyes**
> - Constantly watering eyes
> - Eyes sensitive to light (photophobia)
> - Eyelids burning, red and swollen
> - Eyes stream on coughing
> - Colds and hay fever
> - Bland, watery nasal catarrh
> - Loose cough during day only, better for lying down
> - Eye symptoms accompanying other illnesses, for example colds, measles
> - Catarrhal headaches

Description facts
- This remedy is frequently indicated in allergies and hay fever when there are acrid tears and bland nasal discharge. This is the opposite of *Allium cepa* (*see* page 44). Besides the burning, watery discharge from the eyes, *Euphrasia* can have a thick, acrid, yellow discharge from the eyes.
- A really profuse mucous discharge from the chest and larynx can accompany the cough. The cough is the opposite of the *Phosphorus* cough (*see* page 89) in that it is better for lying down and occurs only in the daytime.
- The person needing *Euphrasia* yawns when walking outdoors in the open air.

Better/worse facts	
Better:	**Worse:**
Cough better when lying down	Sunlight
	Wind
	Warm room
	Light
	Cold worse when lying down

User-friendly facts
This superb remedy brings great joy and relief. It is a particularly useful remedy when indicated in the treatment of eye conditions.

Clinical facts
Allergies, colds, coughs, hay fever, eye inflammations (conjunctivitis), measles, catarrhal headaches..

Danger facts
Nothing significant

FERRUM PHOSPHORICUM (*Ferrum phos*)

Source facts
Phosphate of iron

Chat facts
Ferrum phos was introduced to the homoeopathic Materia Medica by Dr. Schussler (1821–1898). It can be prescribed according to the Schussler theory and it has also been proved homoeopathically. Dr. Schussler, a German doctor and homoeopath, used remedies to treat patients pathologically (that is he treated the effects of the disease rather than the whole symptom picture). He used low potency remedies to treat physiological functions and deficiencies. He based his choice of remedies on a biochemical clinical theory and not necessarily on proving systems.

> **Key facts**
> - **Initial stage** of inflammatory conditions, before pus formation
> - Lacks the anxiety and restlessness of *Aconite* (see page 42) or the intensity of *Belladonna* (see page 51)
> - Tendency to bleed, for example **nosebleeds**, nosebleeds during colds
> - **Bruises easily**
> - Tends to **flush easily** with excitement although the person may look pale at the onset of illnesses
> - Pale mucous membranes
> - Sluggish and weak – easily fatigued
> - Good spirits despite being ill
> - Likes to be alone

Description facts

- As *Belladonna* affects the arterial circulation, *Ferrum phos* affects the venous circulation. Hence this is a remedy for passive and weak states.
- It is useful as a remedy for the first stages of inflammatory disorders, especially of the chest (bronchitis) and the ears. The cough is painful, tickling, hacking and spasmodic. In ear infections the Eustachian tubes are inflamed and this can cause the sensation of deafness.
- The headaches are better on placing a cold cloth on the forehead.
- The sick person has a strong aversion to meat and milk.
- Pallor and redness alternate and the sick person feels weak.

Better/worse facts	
Better:	Worse:
Cold applications	None
Walking around slowly	
Pressure	

User-friendly facts

This remedy is useful at the onset of infections when the condition is not intense enough to warrant *Belladonna*, yet there are elements of flushing and bleeding. It is suitable for a sensitive sick person who does not have the vital energy to develop severe, acute symptoms and yet could go on to develop inflammation of the ears or chest.

Clinical facts
Blood-streaked discharge from the nose, chest infections, colds with flushing in the face, deafness, first stage of inflammatory disorders, middle-ear infection, mild fevers.

Danger facts
Nothing specific

GELSEMIUM (*Gelsemium sempervirens*)
Yellow Jasmine

Source facts
Tincture made from the bark of the root.

Chat facts
Yellow jasmine is a clinging vine, unable to hold itself up without support. By analogy, you can see the weakness aspect of the whole remedy picture both mentally and physically. The Doctrine of Signatures as expounded by the medieval doctor and alchemist, Paracelsus, creates interesting and useful corresponding images but is not to be confused with homoeopathy. The Doctrine of Signatures states that the manner in which the substance appears, grows, behaves, and so on, will give you an indication of its potential in illness. An example of this is the lungwort plant, which has leaves that resemble lungs and is used for pulmonary conditions.

Key facts
- **Dullness, dizziness, drowsiness** and trembling
- Weakness and floppiness, wants to lie down
- Headaches with visual disturbances
- Flu
- No thirst

> **Key facts – continued**
> - Ailments from fright and shock
> - Ailments from **anticipation** and stage fright
> - Face red or pale, eyelids droopy or heavy

Description facts

- *Gelsemium* can easily be understood by remembering how you felt when you last had flu. You feel drowsy, achy, weak and sore – any effort feels 'too much'. There may be a dull headache, often in the nape of the neck, that sometimes extends to droopy, heavy-feeling eyes. There may be sneezing with a watery nasal discharge. Despite a lack of thirst, there may be profuse urination. Together with trembling and chills up and down the back, there is coldness, especially of the feet, but often with a hot head. The flu takes a few days to get going. *Gelsemium* is also a useful remedy for people who don't recover fully and don't feel well after having had flu.

- With the *Gelsemium* headache (this means the type of headache that *Gelsemium* caused in the provings and which will therefore be helped by *Gelsemium*), the neck can often be stiff and painful and the pain can extend up to the forehead and eyes.

- The *Gelsemium* mental state is one of stage fright or nervous anxiety. Many a school child's butterflies, trembly shakiness, fear, diarrhoea and the sense of not being able to remember anything, calm down after taking this remedy. The *Gelsemium* state is a dread of ordeals, like going to the dentist or giving a speech in public. *Gelsemium* is used for the effects of fright, bad news, shocks, or a feeling of shakiness and trembling that feels better for being held (compare *Pulsatilla*, page 93, who needs to be held for comfort). This kind of fright is helped by 'brandy for shock' too.

Better/worse facts	
Better:	Worse:
Rest, quiet	Emotions, ordeals
Warmth, lying in bed, sweating	Shocks, bad news
Urination	Hot, humid weather
Alcoholic drinks	Fog

User-friendly facts

Remember *Gelsemium* for mental and physical prostration and fatigue with infections, and also for mental and physical shakiness with anxiety.

For butterflies before an event, it is often useful to take a dose of *Gelsemium* the night before the event, the morning of the event, and just before the event.

Clinical facts

Anticipatory fear before an event, excess sun, flu, fright and shock, headaches from fear, shocks, vertigo, viral infections.

Danger facts

Meningitis, where there is stiffness of the neck in the very early stages, with a high fever. The sick person is unable to put his chin on his chest.

HEPAR SULPHURIS (*Hepar sulph*)
Calcium sulfide

Source facts

This remedy was an invention of Hahnemann. He originally prepared it by burning the powdered insides of oyster shells with pure flowers of sulphur at white heat in a closed container and then potentizing it.

Chat facts

Hepar sulph is a remedy that affects the nervous system, causing sick people to be oversensitive, both emotionally and physically. These hypersensitive states are often displayed when this remedy is needed. In low potencies, *Hepar sulph* will help the body to discharge, for example open up blocked sinuses and alleviate stuffy colds.

Key facts
- **Hypersensitive**, irritable
- Quarrelsome, impatient
- Overreacts to draughts, cold

> **Key facts – continued**
> - Pain is pricking, sharp or sticking like a **splinter**
> - **Chilly**
> - Better for warmth
> - Croup is improved in a hot, steamy bathroom
> - **Sweat is profuse and offensive**
> - Pus formation, for instance boils

Description facts

- A sick person needing *Hepar sulph* becomes very irritable and very chilly, often just before or with the onset of a sore throat. He walks around closing windows to get rid of draughts, wearing 20 layers of clothing and scarves and sweating profusely and offensively. He lies in bed with the covers up to his nose and doesn't even want his hands sticking out. He may even want a cap on his head.
- He is easily angered and irritated, and impossible to please (*Chamomilla*, *see* page 60). He craves warm drinks and heat. His sore throat feels like a stuck splinter and is unbearable to him. His sinuses are blocked and the slightest touch to his face is unendurable. The boil on his behind is so sensitive that he must lie on his stomach. Even his mother finds it a trifle hard to love him!
- The child in this *Hepar sulph* state wakes up at midnight with croup (*Aconite*, *see* page 42) and by 3 a.m. he and his exhausted parents are sitting in a steamy, hot bathroom, which gives him marked relief.
- The skin is unhealthy and mild cuts become pussy and suppurate. Pus or mucus forms, whether in boils, painful sinuses or tonsils.
- Coughs are rattly and croupy, or barking (*Aconite*, *see* page 42 and *Spongia*, *see* page 103).

User-friendly facts

Hypersensitivity is the thread that runs through this remedy. High potencies of *Hepar sulph* (over a 30ch potency) will stop suppuration, while low potencies help discharge pus or bring a boil to a head.

Aconite (*see* page 42), *Hepar sulph* (*see* page 69) and *Spongia* (*see* page 103) can be rotated every 15 minutes or as needed for the treatment of croup. This is an old tip handed down by Count von Boenninghausen, a famous student of Hahnemann.

Better/worse facts	
Better:	**Worse:**
Warmth	Cold, especially cold air
Moist heat	Dry air
Quiet	Eating or drinking cold food or drinks
	The least uncovering of the body or affected part
	Touch
	Whatever is perceived as irritating

Clinical facts
Boils, catarrh, colds, croup, earache, sinusitis, sore throats, styes, suppuration.

Danger facts
Do not use *Hepar sulph* below a 30ch in acute ear conditions. This is because low potencies cause a discharge and the eardrum will be placed under pressure. Potencies of 30ch or higher will stop suppuration. Where there is a vent, as in a boil, a low potency can safely be used.

See **Croup, Danger facts** in **Cough, Danger facts,** page 137

HYPERICUM (*Hypericum perforatum*)
St John's Wort

Source facts
Potentized tincture of whole fresh plant.

Chat facts
This medicinal plant is called *Hypericum perforatum* because the leaves, when held up to the light, look perforated as a result of the translucent oil glands in the leaf. The oil found in the leaf and flower is red in colour and this led to the name St John's Wort, or Wound, as the oil looks a little like blood. True to its name, it is very useful for the treatment of wounds and woes.

Hypericum has recently taken the world by storm as a remedy for the nervous system in herbal form. Besides its effect of healing nerve injuries in potency, this herb is now used worldwide as a treatment for mild to moderate depression. The latest scientific research shows that it increases the brain's serotonin levels.

> **Key facts**
> - Painfulness and **sensitivity** of the **nerves**
> - **Injury** to nerves, especially fingers and toes
> - Crush injuries
> - Intolerable, violent, shooting, sharp pains
> - Injuries to brain and spinal cord or tailbone (coccyx)
> - Side effects of lumbar punctures and epidural anaesthetics
> - Puncture or penetrating wounds excessively sensitive
> - Animal or insect bites
> - **Neuralgia** (nerve pain)

Description facts
- *Hypericum* is the '*Arnica*' of the nervous system as *Symphytum* (*see* page 105) is the '*Arnica*' of the bones. After an injury to the spine, falling on the tailbone (coccyx) or catching your finger in the car door, *Hypericum* is a great healer. The pains radiate out, causing jerking and twitching and extremely painful sensitivity.
- Neuralgia (nerve pain) with tingling, burning numbness and sciatica from prolonged sitting are relieved by *Hypericum*.
- Antitetanus action, so use it before going for an antitetanus injection (compare *Ledum*, page 79).

User-friendly facts
The tincture and oil are used for the treatment of wounds and sprains. All nerve pain, including that from tooth nerves, is helped by *Hypericum* in potency.

Clinical facts
Afterpains of childbirth, concussion, injuries to nerves, injury to brain or spinal cord, neuralgia (nerve pain), puncture wounds, toothache.

Better/worse facts	
Better:	**Worse:**
Warmth	Injury, concussion
	Shock
	Exertion
	Warmth
	Jarring, touch

Danger facts

All concussions and injuries to the spine should be checked, especially if there is a loss of consciousness.

IGNATIA (*Ignatia amara*)
St Ignatius's Bean

Source facts
A trituration and potentization of the seeds.

Chat facts
The *Ignatia* tree is indigenous to the Philippine islands and China and bears pear-sized fruits with seeds approximately 2.5 cm long. Spanish Jesuits who brought the seeds to Europe in the seventeenth century after seeing their useful properties, named the bean. The seeds were used in Europe for the treatment of gout, cholera, epilepsy and asthma.

Key facts
- Rapid change of mood
- **Sighing** and yawning
- Ailments from **grief**, strain, **disappointed love** and long-continued suppression of emotions
- **Hysterical outbursts**

MATERIA MEDICA

> **Key facts – continued**
> - **Contradictory** and paradoxical symptoms
> - Physical ailments with **emotional causes**
> - Likes to be alone to grieve silently
> - Sympathy makes them feel worse (opposite of *Pulsatilla*, see page 93)
> - Pain in small spots like a nail driven in
> - **Globus hystericus** (sensation of a lump in the throat brought about by emotional upsets)
> - Cramps and spasms

Description facts

- We have all felt the need for this remedy at some stage or another. A child may get a sore throat after hearing his parents fighting, after being reprimanded (unfairly, he feels) or after being frightened. A woman's menstrual cycle can be disturbed by emotional grief or upset. We have all experienced the lump in the throat that won't go away after receiving sad news, after the death of a loved one or even a pet, or after long-continued stress. The sighing and yawning that may also indicate this remedy in the adult shows up as grimaces and facial tics in a child. The person experiencing *Ignatia* grief prefers to be alone to grieve and cry and does not respond well to sympathy.
- Paradoxical or inappropriate emotions are often displayed, for example the desire to giggle at a funeral, laughing and crying at the same time, crying with joy or saying the wrong things at the wrong time.
- Silent or suppressed grief can often lead to hysterical outbursts or to physical ailments. These too can be paradoxical, for example a sore throat that is better for eating, upset stomachs with a desire for rich food, which are easily tolerated, or a cough that gets worse the more you cough.
- There can be headaches from stress or emotions in a small spot on the head, like a nail being driven inwards.

User-friendly facts

This remedy shows the profound effect emotions have on the physical body because of the very intimate and subtle link between mind and body.

Better/worse facts	
Better:	**Worse:**
Passing urine during headaches	Emotions, grief, worry, humiliation, fright, disappointed love
Unusual, unsuitable things like eating toast with a sore throat, or rich foods with bilious attacks	Loss of pets and sentimental objects
Eating	Sympathy
Deep breathing	Odours
	Tobacco and coffee

Clinical facts
Ailments from disappointed love, grief, humiliation, loss of loved ones, pets or sentimental objects, and worry; asthma and insomnia from emotions; cramps, colic, disturbed menstrual cycle, tics.

Danger facts
Nothing significant

IPECACUANHA (*Ipecac*)
Ipecac root

Source facts
Trituration and potency of the dried roots.

Chat facts
Ipecac has a long history of use in medicine. It is utilized to induce vomiting and as an expectorant in cough mixtures. This gives us an insight into the Law of Similars – Like cures like.

> **Key facts**
> - **Constant nausea**, with a **clean tongue**
> - Nausea accompanying complaints
> - Extreme salivation
> - Nausea worse for thought or smell of food
> - Nausea not better for vomiting
> - Sleepiness after vomiting
> - **Bleeding with nausea** profuse, bright and gushing, for example nosebleeds
> - Nosebleeds with cough
> - Cough asthmatic, constricting
> - Gags with violent, incessant cough
> - Sudden bronchitis with profuse bubbly, moist mucus, difficult breathing
> - No thirst

Description facts

- The *Ipecac* sufferer has a severe form of nausea. He is constantly nauseous with a desire to vomit but the nausea is not relieved by vomiting. It is worsened by smelling dinner cooking or even thinking of eating. Strangely, there is no thirst with the nausea and the tongue is clean with profuse salivation. *Ipecac* nausea often goes together with other illnesses, that is it is concomitant.
- A child needing *Ipecac* will take ill suddenly with vomiting. This is soon followed by a constant coughing and sneezing. The next stage is a loud, loose bubbling in the chest that cannot be coughed up but can sometimes be expelled through vomiting.
- There can be a sudden, bright red nosebleed. The child becomes sleepy, irritable, and very difficult and bad-tempered. She often doesn't know what she wants (compare *Chamomilla*, page 60).

User-friendly facts

Nausea can present together with all the complaints or as a symptom on its own.

Clinical facts

Asthma, bleeding, bronchitis, cough, nausea, nosebleeds.

Better/worse facts	
Better:	**Worse:**
Closing eyes	Motion
Open air	Warmth
	Thought or smell of food
	Abuse of drugs, painkillers and anaesthetics

Danger facts
Excessive vomiting.
If mucus becomes suffocative.

KALI BICHROMICUM (*Kali bich*)
Potassium bichromate

Source facts
The solution of this chemical in cold water, potentized.

Chat facts
This remedy was first proved in 1844 after it was noticed that the workers who prepared and used this salt suffered from many ailments. This salt is widely used in art for dyeing and staining, and also in electric batteries.

Key facts
- Discharges from mucous membranes
- **Thick, yellow-green, stringy** discharges
- Nasal crusts
- Pain and infection in sinuses
- **Postnasal discharges**
- Pain felt in circumscribed small spots
- **Ulcers**, punched out on skin and in mouth

> **Key facts – continued**
> - Pains changing location rapidly
> - Croupy, metallic coughs
> - Migraines with visual disturbance

Description facts

- The sinus and nasal symptom pictures of *Kali bich* are commonly seen and very specific. The mucous discharge is most distinctive and consists of a thick, yellow-green discharge from the nose and chest that is so sticky that it can be pulled into strings. Some of the mucus is lumpy and forms hard crusts.
- The postnasal drip is thick and difficult to swallow or spit out and can cause an irritated sore throat, often in the morning on waking. A warm drink relieves the throat pain. If you look at the throat, you will find the little tongue (uvula) to be swollen and oedematous and you will often notice two strings of thick yellow mucus hanging down the back of the throat. The throat pain is worse if you protrude the tongue. The tongue is thickly coated and broad. The mouth feels sticky and it may feel as if there is a hair on the back part of the tongue.
- The blocked or obstructed nose is often accompanied by pain in the bridge or root of the nose. The pain of the blocked or infected sinuses can be severe and is often accompanied by a headache that feels like a solid block in the forehead. The headache feels worse if you stoop or bend forward. These sinus headaches can be caused by catarrh that is suppressed by medication or is just very thick. Thus it stagnates and can become infected within the sinus cavities. There is often a loss of the sense of smell.
- Another type of *Kali bich* headache often starts with flickering visual disturbances in front of the eyes. The pain is felt in circumscribed spots on the head. Pressure on these spots gives a little relief.
- The cough is metallic or croupy and is caused by a postnasal drip. There can be a catarrhal laryngitis (inflammation of the larynx or voicebox caused by the irritation of the postnasal discharge).

User-friendly facts

This is a most useful remedy covering many sinus and **end-of-cold complaints** where the catarrh or mucus is causing the problems. By reducing the excessive mucus formation, you can prevent frequent re-infections of colds and upper respiratory complaints.

Better/worse facts

Better:	Worse:
Warm drinks	2–3 a.m.
Heat	Protruding the tongue
Pressure	Beer
	Suppressed catarrh
	Stooping
	Eating, which causes cough

Clinical facts

Catarrh, colds, coughs, crusts in nose, ear infections, hay fever, headaches, postnasal discharge, sinusitis.

Danger facts

See **Cough, Danger facts**, page 137

LEDUM (*Ledum palustre*)

Marsh tea, Wild rosemary

Source facts

Tincture and potency of whole plant and dried small twigs, collected after flowering.

Chat facts

The tincture of this plant has been used to treat infestations of lice and other parasites. It is used in the tanning industry, and also has the strange ability to increase the intoxicating power of beer!

> **Key facts**
> - **Puncture wounds**, animal and insect **bites**, needles, splinters
> - Wounded parts are cold
> - Coldness, but **better for cold** applications (even ice)
> - Injury to eye, often with haemorrhage (*Symphytum, see* page 105)
> - Long-lasting bruise discoloration after injury

Description facts

- *Ledum* should be used routinely to prevent complications in puncture wounds. The puncture wounds requiring *Ledum* are often deep with little bleeding. They can range from insect bites that become swollen and inflamed to standing on a drawing pin. The puncture wound can often be very painful.
- *Ledum* is excellent as a remedy for 'black eyes' from a blow. Remember *Symphytum* if the eyeball is painful.

Better/worse facts	
Better:	Worse:
Cold or ice	Heat or warmth in any form

User-friendly facts

This remedy must be thought of for puncture wounds and their long-term effects. Remember it for **spider and tick bites**.

Clinical facts

Bites, black eye, puncture wounds, stings, vaccinations, wounds.

Danger facts

It is essential to have an antitetanus injection after bad wounds or bites.

MAGNESIA PHOSPHORICA (*Mag phos*)

Source facts
A trituration and potency of *Magnesia phosphorica*.

Chat facts
This substance was originally introduced to the homoeopathic pharmacopoeia by Schussler, who used it in his tissue salts.

> **Key facts**
> - **Neuralgic pains, relieved by warmth**
> - **Colic** relieved by warmth, bending, **rubbing** and passing flatus (wind)
> - **Cramping** of muscles
> - Toothache better for warm drinks
> - Pain in irritable, teething children
> - Headaches

Description facts
- This remedy is similar to *Colocynthis* (*see* page 62). The *Mag phos* sufferers like the warmth and gentle pressure of a hot-water bottle, or the gentle pressure of rubbing. This is a significant difference from the hard pressure liked by *Colocynthis* sufferers. *Mag phos* is anxious and tense unlike the irritable *Colocynthis*. There is also a strong neuralgic component that is brought on by cold water and cold air and is improved by warmth.
- Wherever the pain, cramp or neuralgia (nerve pain) is located, *Mag phos* will be of value if warmth and gentle pressure or rubbing alleviates the symptoms.

User-friendly facts
This remedy is a superb antispasmodic.

Clinical facts
Colic, cramps (all types), headaches, neuralgia (nerve pain), pain, period pains, toothache.

Better/worse facts	
Better:	**Worse:**
Warmth	Cold and cold air
Gentle pressure	Cold wind
Rubbing	
Doubling up	
Passing flatus	

Danger facts
See Colocynthis, page 62

MERCURIUS SOLUBLIS HAHNEMANNI (*Merc sol*)

Source facts
This is made from the soluble black oxide of mercury by the process of trituration.

Chat facts
Merc sol is another example of how a toxic substance like mercury, through trituration and dilution, can become a safe medication. It is easy to remember that mercury is used in thermometers and barometers for its ability to react to the weather. In the *Merc sol* remedy picture, this too can be seen. Although highly toxic, it has a long historical use for the treatment of syphilis and degenerative conditions.

> **Key facts**
> - **Hypersensitive to both heat and cold** – hot one minute and cold the next
> - **Increased saliva** and **dribbling** while sleeping, often with intense thirst for cold water, fizzy drinks or milk
> - Perspiration profuse, offensive and does not relieve the condition
> - Restlessness with weakness; a trembling feeling internally

> **Key facts – continued**
> - Flabby, slimy tongue indented with tooth marks along the edge
> - **Offensive breath**, discharges and perspiration
> - Swollen lymph glands
> - Sore throat extending to the ears and chest
> - Night aggravations
> - A desire to pass urine or stool that continues after urination or diarrhoea

Description facts

- To help you understand the *Merc sol* picture, we will describe an extreme case of a *Merc sol* sore throat (that is the symptoms that *Merc sol* has will correspond to both the sore throat and the sick person's reaction to it).
- The sick person has creeping chills alternating with fevers that are hot and cold and covers and uncovers himself all night. He aches in his bones, especially at night. He sweats easily and profusely, but it brings no relief. The sweat can be offensive. On the pillow is a little moist patch dribbled in his sleep.
- The lymph glands are swollen. On opening the mouth the sick person has a wet, slimy, flabby, indented tongue with offensive breath or halitosis. The throat or tonsils can be inflamed and often have small pustular areas on them. The tonsils are enlarged. In spite of all this moisture, the sick person is often very thirsty for cold liquids and likes to eat ice or ice cream. He is restless, irritable and weak and feels trembly inside. He definitely feels worse at night.
- *Merc sol* also has frequent chest infections with yellow-green expectoration.
- Aching sinuses with pain that extends to the teeth is a sure-fire prescription for *Merc sol*. The nasal discharge can be yellow-green.
- The gums can be inflamed, bleeding and spongy, and mouth ulcers are common. There may be inflammation of the eyes (conjunctivitis) with a burning, acrid discharge, often before a cold starts.
- During a cold there is a lot of sneezing with profuse watery discharge that is worse in the sun and in time becomes yellow-green.
- Bladder infections (cystitis) with urging continuing after passing urine respond to *Merc sol*.
- Diarrhoea with slimy, offensive, green, bloody stools and continued urging.

Better/worse facts	
Better:	**Worse:**
Rest	Heat and cold
Daytime	Change in weather
	Open air
	Night
	Sweating
	Draughts

User-friendly facts
Bear in mind that you do not need to have all the symptoms to use *Merc sol* successfully. Also remember that *Merc sol* is quicksilver, the human barometer, and is sensitive to all little changes in temperature and weather.

Clinical facts
Chest infections, cystitis, diarrhoea, earache, eye inflammation (conjunctivitis), inflammation of throat and tonsils, mouth ulcers, mumps, sinusitis, swelling of glands, unhealthy gums.

Danger facts
For **Fever** and **Throats** *see* **Fever, Danger facts**, page 162 and **Sore throats, Danger facts**, page 189

NATRUM MURIATICUM (*Nat mur*)
Common rock salt

Source facts
Dilution and potentization of this salt.

Chat facts
This is an example of how a common item of diet and the main constituent of tears can become an invaluable and deep-acting remedy through the homoeopathic process of

dilution and succussion. It is well known that an excessive intake of salt is bad for the health, causing high blood pressure, kidney problems and fluid retention. By taking the homoeopathic potency of *Nat mur* you can often reduce the craving for table salt.

> **Key facts**
> - Desire to be **alone,** especially if stressed or grieved
> - Ailments from **grief**
> - Worse for consolation but desires empathy
> - **Headaches hammering** and recurring, often with flickering vision and spots in front of eyes
> - Migraines and blinding headaches
> - Worse at 10 a.m.
> - Worse for sun and heat of sun
> - Desire for **salt**, **water**, garlic and bitter substances, e.g. beer or tonic water
> - Urticaria (hives)
> - Mapped tongue, also known as a geographical tongue, with patches of red and white coatings on the tongue
> - Colds and hay fever beginning with violent sneezing and with a watery discharge from eyes and nose, often like the raw white of an egg
> - Blocked nose when nose is not running
> - Loss of smell and taste

Description facts

- A sick person needing *Nat mur* for grief is often unable to cry at the appropriate time and may laugh instead of weeping (compare *Ignatia*, page 73). She weeps when she is alone or may find herself crying while watching dog food commercials on television. She wishes to be alone to mull over her thoughts and understand the meaning of what may have occurred. Unfortunately she often gets into a mode of repetitive thinking like an old record that gets stuck in a groove. She dwells on her grief and on all pains from the past, becoming quietly resentful inside. She doesn't want to be consoled especially by superficial company and often suffers silently. She escapes into reading, often science fiction and 'bodice-ripper' books that will distract her. She becomes sleepless after grief.

- The headaches of *Nat mur* are severe, throbbing and often blinding, both in the intensity of the pain and from the visual disturbances of spots, flickering, zigzags and partial loss of vision. The headaches can be caused by exposure to the sun. They often begin on waking or at 10 a.m.

Better/worse facts	
Better:	Worse:
Cool, open air	9–11 a.m.
Cool bathing	Sun
Lying on a hard surface	
Sea (some people will generally feel better at the beach, others not)	

User-friendly facts

If you are under professional homoeopathic treatment and have been prescribed *Nat mur* in a high potency as a constitutional remedy, please check with your homoeopath before using *Nat mur* as a first-aid remedy or in tissue salt form as it may act as an antidote and thus interfere with your treatment.

Clinical facts

Colds, grief and its effects, hay fever, headaches, migraines, urticaria.

Danger facts

If you have never suffered from migraines and get a sudden, severe headache with partial loss of vision, seek professional help.

NUX VOMICA (*Nux vom*)
Strychnos nux vomica, Poison-nut

Source facts

Tincture and titruration of the seeds. This tree produces flowers with an unpleasant odour in winter. This is quite opposite to pleasant-smelling plants flowering in spring and is indicative of the contrary nature of the chilly, irritable person needing *Nux vom*.

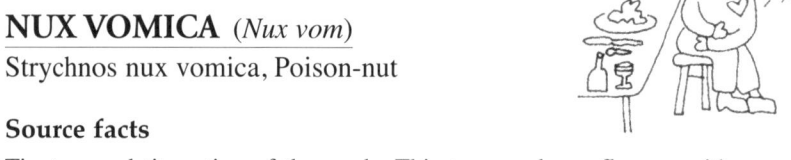

Chat facts

A wonderful remedy for all ailments that cause irritability due to stress. It helps you to make a transition from stress to relaxation and recuperation.

Key facts
- **Irritability, impatience**
- **Sensitive** to touch, pain, smell, **noise**, music, drugs
- Overworked and **overstressed**
- Frequent ineffectual urge for urine and stool, feels that it is 'never quite finished'
- Stomach problems from overeating, junk, or fastfood eating
- Nausea, heartburn
- **Hunger** with all ailments
- Craves spices, fats, alcohol, coffee, tasty food
- For the bad effects of excess drugs and alcohol
- Wakes 3–5 a.m. with an active, **anxious, worrying mind**
- **Chilly**
- Spasms

Description facts

- A *Nux vom* man, after an exhausting but stimulating work week, during which his third secretary of the year resigned because of his critical, perfectionist outbursts, went out for a business dinner. At the traffic light he had to hoot at the slowness of the traffic, swearing under his breath at their stupidity. After four courses of food, including a curry and three different wines, he had a cognac and cigar as a nightcap. To his surprise he reacted as he had to his greasy Sunday barbecue, with nausea, heartburn and a hangover headache. If only he could vomit, he thought he might feel better instead of suffering from his crampy stomach and passing little bits of stool frequently. He was very cold and irritable, and the noise of the puppy next door seemed unbearable.
- He fell asleep in front of the television and woke at 3 a.m. worrying about business. He got up and tidied his papers and his room, angrily. He made a cup of coffee and put on the heater and finally fell into an exhausted sleep at 5 a.m., only to be awoken by his alarm clock at 6 a.m. Poor secretary, poor wife, poor dog!

- Although our example is of a *Nux vom* male, a *Nux vom* female exists too, especially before her period, when her whole family, and even the dog, know to avoid her sarcastic comments and irritable nature!
- *Nux vom* has a rough, dry, tickling sore throat. This is often accompanied by a drippy, sneezy cold in the day and a blocked nose at night. *Nux vom* is one of the most useful hay fever remedies.
- As we have tried to show you, *Nux vom* is irritable, chilly and perfectionist. He will neaten up papers and make the paintings hang straight. (*Ars alb*, see page 49, and *Silicea*, see page 101, are also very perfectionist about small details).

Better/worse facts	
Better:	**Worse:**
Undisturbed, unbroken sleep, naps	Long mental or emotional stress
Hot drinks, warmth	3–5 a.m.
Vomiting, stool or any elimination	Cold, open air, draught and wind
Firm pressure, rubbing	Coffee, condiments, drugs, purgatives, laxatives
	Sedentary habits
	Overeating, overdrinking, overplaying
	Too much mental exertion and fatigue
	Overreaction to almost everything, like pain, noise, bright light, anger, pressure of clothes

User-friendly facts

As you can see, this remedy is ideal for a sick person suffering from prolonged stress and inability to relax, as well as the stress and indulgences of our modern life. A person needing *Nux vom* cannot get his nervous system to change from 'Fright and Flight' to 'Rest and Recuperation' mode and becomes depleted and worn out. A good example of this is a student who studies until very late at night and then can't switch his mind off to relax and go to sleep.

Nux vom is also useful for those people who are always cleaning out their livers with all kinds of preparations or their bowels with laxatives.

Clinical facts
Constipation, cramping (stomach, menstrual, and so on), effects of excess alcohol, food indiscretions, hangovers, hay fever, heartburn, insomnia, irritability before periods, nausea, piles, sore throats, seasickness, tantrums.

Danger facts
Nothing significant.

PHOSPHORUS (*Phosphorus*)

Source facts
Trituration and potentization of the red amorphous *Phosphorus*.

Chat facts
Phosphorus is an essential element for both animal and plant life and particularly important for building strong bones and teeth. Because it is widely used in fizzy cold drinks as phosphoric acid, it is easy for an excess to be ingested, causing an imbalance and excretion of calcium, which is necessary for strong teeth and bones. This helps to highlight the dangers of excessive intake of cold drinks.

When exposed to air, phosphorus metal bursts into flame and burns with lots of light and no heat. *Phosphorus* is an example of a remedy that can be prescribed constitutionally or for the symptomatic imbalance of young people who grow too thin, tall and quickly and easily lose their fizz.

> **Key facts**
> - **Craves** and needs **sympathy** and physical **affection**, touch and **rubbing**
> - Anxious and doesn't like to be left alone
> - **Fears** of the **dark**, **ghosts**, twilight, thunderstorms
> - Desires ice cold drinks and **ice cream**, salty, spicy, tasty food and chocolate
> - Burning pains
> - Tends to bleed easily from wounds
> - Colds go to the chest (*Merc sol*, see page 82)

> **Key facts – continued**
> - Weak, tight chest with easy coughs
> - Nausea and gastric pain, better for cold drinks that are vomited up as soon as they warm up in the stomach
> - Palpitations with anxiety

Description facts

- The person or child needing *Phosphorus* has a tight chest with a minor cough. If she can, she will sit next to or on her mother, needing constant reassurance and not wanting to be left alone. She usually craves cold drinks, ice or ice cream (or chocolates and chips), but with a bad chest sometimes prefers warm drinks. She needs to sit up when coughing and needs many pillows to lean against, as the cough is worse when she lies down flat. In the later stages the cough becomes loose and she can cough up greenish-yellow, sometimes blood-streaked mucus. The cough is often painful, with burning in the chest or pain behind the breastbone. After being in a warm room, cold air makes the need to cough much worse, as does talking or laughing.
- *Phosphorus* easily becomes hoarse or develops laryngitis that is especially bad in the early evening and renders the sick person unable to speak. The tickling in the larynx leads to coughs. Sometimes she can experience painless laryngitis and a total loss of voice.
- A person needing *Phosphorus* is unable to lie on her left side, and can easily develop nosebleeds.
- She can experience pain and burning in the stomach. The pain is better for eating and she craves cold drinks that help the pain briefly until the liquid warms in the stomach. She regurgitates undigested food.
- The diarrhoea can be exhausting but painless and can become involuntary with traces of blood.
- With the typical *Phosphorus* anxiety, she has palpitations that obviously make her even more anxious and she needs someone to be with her and reassure her.
- She often bleeds excessively from minor incidents, for instance dental extraction, cuts and injuries. She is better for short sleeps and feels awful if deprived of sleep.

Better/worse facts	
Better:	**Worse:**
Cold drinks, cold food	Lying flat or on left side
Warmth	Sensitive to emotions, external impressions
Sympathy, company, massage	Twilight, thunderstorms, darkness
Sitting up	Warm food and drink
	Being alone

User-friendly facts

Anxiety always seems to accompany *Phosphorus* conditions. The chest weakness is a key factor in acute conditions that need *Phosphorus*. This remedy is frequently indicated when colds and flu go to the chest.

Clinical facts

Anxiety, bleeding, bronchitis, chest infections, coughs, diarrhoea, indigestion, inflammation of stomach, laryngitis, nausea, nosebleeds.

Danger facts

Phosphorus 6ch or lower should not be repeated for too many days, as overuse could cause a proving in susceptible people and thus cause bleeding. The 30ch is perfectly safe.

PODOPHYLLUM (*Podophyllum peltatum*)
May apple, American mandrake

Source facts
Potentized tincture of the root gathered after the fruit has ripened.

Chat facts
The egg-shaped fruit looks like a small lemon. It has been used by native Americans to expel worms and to cure deafness. The juice has also been used, in its crude form, to burn off warts.

> **Key facts**
> - **Diarrhoea** – profuse, **explosive**, **gushing**, green-yellow or watery brown, painless and offensive
> - Diarrhoea with teething
> - Rumbling and **gurgling** before stool
> - Complaints accompanied by diarrhoea, for example headaches, teething
> - Gastric flu

Description facts

- A baby may need *Podophyllum* while teething. Teething is characterized by a great desire to press the gums together – this is known as dentition diarrhoea. The baby's head sweats during sleep and he will often have diarrhoea while being bathed. The profuse, gushing diarrhoea soaks through the nappy. There are often gurgling sounds in the abdomen just before another gush of explosive diarrhoea. Remember that the diarrhoea can also be involuntary while asleep. Adults and children respond well to this wonderful remedy.

Better/worse facts	
Better:	Worse:
Pressure	Early morning
Lying on the abdomen	Eating and drinking
Lying down	Dentition
	Motion
	Hot weather

User-friendly facts

The profuseness and noisiness of this diarrhoea make the choice of *Podophyllum* as a remedy hard to miss.

Clinical facts

Diarrhoea, teething.

DANGER FACTS

If the diarrhoea persists or there is a chance of dehydration, seek professional help and rehydrate the sufferer.

PULSATILLA (*Pulsatilla nigricans*)
Anemone, Windflower

Source facts
Tincture of the entire fresh flower.

Chat facts
This purple flower from the Ranunculaceae family flowers in spring and autumn. Its head hangs down shyly and moves with every breeze. This has led to its being called the 'windflower'. These characteristics, symbolic of its shy and changeable nature, became evident when this delicate flower was potentized and proved. It has been used in medicine since ancient times for many different purposes. Hahnemann says of *Pulsatilla*: 'This powerful plant produces many symptoms on the healthy human body which often correspond to the marked symptoms commonly met with, hence, also, they admit of frequent homoeopathic employment and often do good. It is thereby unquestionably reckoned as a remedy of many uses or a polycrest. It is useful in acute as well as chronic diseases. The homoeopathic employment of this is most suitable when not only the physical symptoms of the remedy correspond in similarity to the physical symptoms of the disease, but also when the mental and emotional disorders peculiar to the drug encounter similar states in the disease to be cured.'

Key facts
- **Changeable** symptoms and moods
- Moody, tearful, **vulnerable**
- Whining and clinging children
- Craves **company** and attention
- Easily consoled
- Discharges **thick, yellow-green, bland**

> **Key facts – continued**
> - Can be chilly, but **needs fresh air**
> - Sensitive to hot stuffy rooms
> - Gets ill when feet are cold and wet
> - **No thirst** even with fever
> - Better for **moving around** or being carried around slowly
> - One cheek is red and the other one pale

Description facts

- Once upon a time, the *Pulsatilla* family went to a party and ate too much of the delicious rich foods, ice cream and creamy desserts. As they walked home there was a sudden spring shower and they got their feet wet. On arriving home, the *Pulsatilla* baby vomited up all the party food. She refused even a sip of water and cried constantly if she was not being carried around and consoled.
- The *Pulsatilla* father started belching and had diarrhoea. He felt too sick to carry the baby, complained of a headache and demanded cold, wet cloths for his forehead, the fan on, the heater off, the window open and would like the *Pulsatilla* mother's full and undivided attention.
- Meanwhile the baby continued to whine, started to pull on her ear and wanted to be carried about constantly. She also wanted a cool cloth over her ear. Her face was flushed on one side only, which was the same side as the sore ear.
- The *Pulsatilla* father had more diarrhoea and was very worried as this time it was a different colour from the last stool. He walked around, but felt too ill to carry the baby. In fact, to the *Pulsatilla* mother it felt as if he also wished to be carried!
- The next day the *Pulsatilla* baby and mother woke up with colds, with coughs and thick yellow mucus. The mother also felt premenstrual and after being summoned repeatedly by the *Pulsatilla* father for all sorts of attention, she burst into tears and phoned her mother for help and sympathy.
- Her baby had a runny nose so she put him on her hip and walked slowly around the garden, weeping and worrying about why her menstrual period was late. Then she remembered her *Homoeopathy for the home* book and administered *Pulsatilla* frequently to herself and her family. By the time her mother had flown in to answer the cries for help, the *Pulsatilla* family were busy living happily ever after!

Better/worse facts	
Better:	**Worse:**
Cool open air	Warm, stuffy rooms
Cold applications	Lying down
Cold food or drinks (if they drink, because they often have no thirst)	Getting feet wet
Company, attention, consolation and sympathy	Twilight
	Rich food, fat, ice cream, pork
Moving around slowly	Sun

User-friendly facts

- As you can see in the *Pulsatilla* story, the **Better/worse facts** (modalities) and moods are very important when prescribing this remedy.
- It is often used for measles or viral infections with a nondescript pink-red rash.
- Despite the *Pulsatilla* dislike of and aggravation from fatty, greasy foods, *Pulsatilla* children will often eat butter straight from the dish.
- Often has complaints on one side of the body only.
- A menstrual period is easily delayed from swimming or getting wet.
- Remember to add *Pulsatilla* to your fever remedies where the main characteristics are chilliness, no thirst, a desire for consolation and being worse for warmth.

Clinical facts

Colds and flu, diarrhoea, earaches, emotional and weepy moods, eye inflammations (conjunctivitis), gastric disturbances from dietary indiscretions, headaches, measles, sinusitis.

Danger facts

Nothing significant

RHUS TOXICODENDRON (*Rhus tox*)
Poison oak, Poison ivy

Source facts
Potentized tincture of fresh plant, gathered at sunset and just before the flowers develop.

Chat facts
The allergic reaction to poison ivy that causes blistering and inflamed skin on contact in susceptible people, is well known and gives us an insight into the use of *Rhus tox* in homoeopathy. The peculiarity of this plant is that its poisonous effects are increased during the night, when it is bursting into leaf or when there is no sunshine. The increase of *Rhus tox* symptoms at night and in damp weather can also be seen as reflections of its attributes.

Key facts
- Extreme **restlessness**
- Worse for cold, damp weather
- Affects skin with chickenpox-like itchy, **watery blisters**
- Skin eruptions better for heat
- Fibrous tissue affected from overstrain or cold, damp weather
- Pain and stiffness with great need to move
- Pain **worse for rest**, initial first movement and overexertion
- Pain **better for continued movement** and limbering up
- **Overexertion** leads to a return of the pain and easy fatigue
- Pain from lifting heavy objects or sprains to ligaments
- Ailments from getting wet
- Lower back pain (lumbago) from lifting heavy objects, strains better lying on a hard surface
- Tongue coated, with clear red triangle at tip
- Flu with restless aches and pains
- Desire for cold milk

Description facts
- To describe the myriad uses of this polycrest remedy, we will tell you the dramatic saga of the camping holiday of the *Rhus tox* family.
- One bright sunny day, the *Rhus tox* family decides to go away for a camping weekend in the country. The *Rhus tox* father wishes to be near some hot mineral baths as he has always been prone to a touch of rheumatism. They arrive at the perfect spot, set up camp and start the fire for a nice barbecue.
- His son wanders off to explore the terrain. They hear him crying and rush off to find him sitting on the ground scratching furiously at his leg. He has had an allergic reaction to some plant that he brushed against. His leg has swollen, is red and covered with little water blisters. For a moment the *Rhus tox* mother wonders if he has caught chickenpox, but the rest of his body is clear. He is sure that he has been poisoned and that he will soon die. He is very anxious and restless, and nothing will satisfy him but a hot bath. Unfortunately the hot mineral baths are closed for the night. To pacify him they warm a glass of milk for him, but he refuses it and will only have it cold. He is so restless that the *Rhus tox* mother can't get him to sit still while she looks for her homoeopathic first-aid kit which is still packed away. How she wishes that she had read through the entire book before going away. Eventually, however, she gives him a dose of *Rhus tox* and is amazed by how rapidly the itching improves. She continues to give it to him until he falls into a deep, restful sleep.
- The *Rhus tox* teenager refuses to help and is not one bit interested in her brother's woes. She lies stretched out in the sun 'working on her tan'. By nightfall she is red, hot and blistered and has a *Belladonna* headache (throbbing and feverish, *see* page 51). Her skin feels sensitive to the cold air and she is restless and achy. Alas, there is no hot bath for her to monopolize and she is very anxious that her blisters will leave her scarred forever. *Rhus tox* comes to the rescue again.
- The *Rhus tox* family settles down for the night, only to be woken in the morning by water dripping into and onto their tent. The weather has turned cold and it is raining heavily. The *Rhus tox* father stiffly gets up out of his sleeping bag and needs to stretch and slowly loosen up. How he hates the damp as it always aggravates his rheumatism. He starts to pack up camp in the pouring rain and in his efforts to hurry tries to carry too many things to the car at once. Oh no! Suddenly his back goes and he can't lift one more thing. Yet again knowledge gained from *Homoeopathy for the home* comes to the rescue. He is so grateful

for the relief of pain. He keeps telling his wife how clever he was to have bought her *Homoeopathy for the home* for Christmas.

- The *Rhus tox* mother finishes off packing the car and gets soaked in the process. She gratefully jumps into the car to get warm and longs to be home and in a hot bath. The next morning she wakes up with the flu, feeling stiff, aching and very restless. She cannot keep her legs still and feels too stiff to lie in bed. It is impossible to find a comfortable position in which to lie. Everything feels worse when she tries to move, but if she continues to move around, the aching improves for a while. Her hot-water bottle doesn't stay warm for long enough and she feels a dry, tickling cough starting.

- The *Rhus tox* father suggests she takes the same remedy that helped his back and their son's skin. She tries to explain to him the principle that each remedy must fit the individual symptom picture in homoeopathy, but is then amazed to find that *Rhus tox* works for her too.

Better/worse facts	
Better:	**Worse:**
Continued movement	Rest
Lying on hard surfaces	At night, and from not moving at night
Warmth	Initial movement
Rubbing	Rising from sitting
Hot baths	Overexertion, overstrain
	Damp
	Being chilled after being heated or perspiring

User-friendly facts
The modalities of the effects of movement and warmth are so well defined that they will lead you clearly to *Rhus tox*. Please reread the remedy *Bryonia* (*see* page 53) to note the opposite modalities.

Clinical facts
Chickenpox, effects of overexertion, sprains and strains, flu, herpes, injuries to ankles, back, ligaments, muscles and joints, urticaria.

Danger facts
Nothing significant.

RUTA GRAVEOLENS (*Ruta*)
Garden rue

Source facts
Potencies are made from the whole plant gathered before the flowers develop.

Chat facts
This ancient herb has been used for millennia in herbalism. Shakespeare mentions it in Richard III. It is sometimes known as 'the herb of grace', and a bunch of rue was commonly used by priests for ritual sprinkling and purification. It inhibits the activities of fleas, lice and other insects.

> **Key facts**
> - **Sprains** accompanied with lameness and **slow healing**
> - Injured or bruised bones
> - Pain as if bruised or lame
> - Aching with restlessness
> - Eyestrain
> - Complaints of the **ankles**, **wrists**, **cartilaginous** tissue in the body
> - Ganglions
> - Repetitive strain injuries, for example overuse of computer keyboards
> - Spot-pain at point where tendon attaches to bone
> - Contraction of **tendons**
> - Injuries to flexor muscles from lifting very heavy objects

Description facts
- This remedy is of great use in repetitive strain injuries, for instance sporting injuries, use of computer keyboards,etc. Carpenters, musicians and players on

one-armed bandits are also prone to such injuries. The sprains are always accompanied by great weakness of the joints. There is a tendency for the sprains to injure the point where the tendons join the periosteum (the sensitive membranous lining around the bone). This causes a pain in a 'spot' and makes *Ruta* a very useful remedy in bruising of the bones (*Arnica*, *see* page 47, has bruising of the soft tissue). The pains of *Ruta* are bruised and aching with a feeling of restlessness and are always better for movement.

- The person needing *Ruta* has a back pain from injuries, sprains, or from her 'back going out' and this is accompanied by a weak, bruised feeling.
- *Ruta* has a specific effect on the muscles of the eye. It relieves painful eyes caused by eyestrain and can strengthen eye muscles and improve vision. Neither of us wears glasses yet as a result of taking *Ruta* 6ch daily over a long period of time!

Better/worse facts	
Better:	**Worse:**
Warmth	Stooping
Motion	Cold, wet
	Rest, lying down
	Overexertion, overuse
	Lying on the painful part
	Eye strain

User-friendly facts
Ruta does not have the element of fatigue that sets in with *Rhus tox* (*see* page 96). In injuries to the joints it is often well indicated after the use of *Rhus tox* to complete the healing.

Clinical facts
After effects of fractures, back pain, bruising, bruising and injury of bone and cartilage, dislocation and sprains of joints, eyestrain, ganglions, injury to small joints.

Danger facts
Nothing specific.

SILICEA (*Silicea*)
Silicon dioxide, Quartz

Source facts
This inert and insoluble substance has been turned into a most useful and active medication using trituration and potentization.

Chat facts
There is an abundance of silica in the earth, in many minerals and crystals and in the stems of plants. Both cement and glass contain large quantities of silica. It is necessary to provide the strength to hold up plants, and in our bodies for healthy skin, hair, nails and connective tissue. In the modern world, we know of its use in a computer's microchips.

A person needing *Silicea* constitutionally will pay attention to the minutest details, and can be compared to the silicon chips in a computer that are also minutely detailed. However, he exhibits a lack of self-confidence and physical strength as a plant stem would without its silica. The *Silicea* patient can be as obstinate as cement and as fragile (emotionally) as glass.

Constitutional treatment must never be confused with acute or first-aid work. The former is aimed at changing or improving the basic susceptibility of an individual and should be undertaken by a professional homoeopath only.

Key facts
- **Pus formation** on tonsils and ears
- Injuries and sores with **slow healing** and festering
- **Expels** foreign bodies, for example splinters
- Perspires on hands, feet or head, and perspiration is offensive
- **Chilly**, wants to be covered with scarf and hat
- Worse for any draught of air or chill, especially on head
- Headaches
- Feels very sensitive, weepy and needy
- Can be obstinate
- Anticipatory anxiety

Description facts

- A sensitive student becomes a perfectionist, lost in the details of her work, anxious and anticipates disasters such as failing or not doing well enough. Her courage fails her and she can often become ill before the event.
- *Silicea* is often the remedy for a painful ear, after you have needed to use *Belladonna* (*see* page 51), *Hepar sulph* (*see* page 69) or *Pulsatilla* (*see* page 93). The sick person is not as sensitive to touch as *Hepar sulph*, but often covers the ear to keep it warm (in contrast to *Pulsatilla*). The pain is made worse by noise and the ear feels blocked. If the eardrum has perforated naturally or if a child has grommets, *Silicea* will help drain and clear the discharge.
- Often the ear infection occurs at the same time as a sore throat, or tonsillitis with pus formation. There may also be sinusitis with this upper respiratory infection. Much thick mucus is discharged postnasally and this continues for a long time.
- Despite being very chilly, the child likes to drink cold drinks and eat cold foods.
- *Silicea* headaches are quite distinctive. They can be severe and caused by stress or not eating regularly. The pain begins in the neck or back of the head (occiput) and spreads over the head, settling over the eyes, usually on the left. The pain can be relieved by profuse urination (*Gelsemium*, *see* page 67), or by warmth to the head or neck (*Mag phos*, *see* page 81). Everything else makes it worse!
- When a boil is no longer as acute as *Belladonna* or *Hepar sulph*, or refuses to come to a head, frequent and repeated use of *Silicea* will cause it to discharge and heal.
- When *Silicea* is needed, every small injury seems to become infected. The nails may have white spots and be brittle and break or flake easily. Whitlows (any pussy inflammation of the end of a finger or toe, near the nail) that have been treated with *Belladonna* and *Hepar sulph* often require *Silicea* to complete the cure.

Better/worse facts	
Better:	Worse:
Warm room, warmth and wrapping up head	Cold air and draughts, damp
Heat, humidity	Jarring of coccyx

User-friendly facts
As you can see, *Silicea* is often required as a remedy after the initial energetic phase of infection has passed but resolution and healing have not taken place properly.

Clinical facts
Anticipatory anxiety, boils, dental abscesses, earaches, hay fever, injuries, sinusitis, sore throats, splinters.

Danger facts
As mentioned in Chat facts (*see* page 101), constitutional treatment should only be undertaken by a professional homoeopath, so take care not to confuse this with acute or first-aid treatment.

Do not use *Silicea* in a potency lower than a 30ch if the pus has no outlet, for instance for a tooth abscess or an infected ear with an intact eardrum.

If the area around a splinter becomes red and swollen with red streaks extending up the limb, the infection has spread to the lymphatic system and help should be sought.

SPONGIA TOSTA (*Spongia*)
Roasted sponge

Source facts
Potentized tincture of *Spongia*.

Chat facts
Sponges have been used since antiquity to treat goitres, as they contain large quantities of iodine and many other minerals. The roasting process used in the manufacture of this remedy releases these minerals.

> **Key facts**
> - Dryness of mucous membranes
> - Hacking, harsh, hollow, **barking, dry, croupy coughs**
> - Croup worse before midnight

> **Key facts – continued**
> - Anxiety and difficulty breathing
> - Wakes around midnight with fear of suffocation
> - Coughs from talking and dry, cold winds
> - Cough **improved by drinking warm drinks** or eating
> - Hoarseness with coughs, colds and laryngitis
> - Difficult breathing better for bending forward
> - Laryngitis with very sensitive throat that can be triggered by touch on throat or turning the head

Description facts

- A *Spongia* attack, usually seen in children, occurs around midnight with anxiety, a fear of not being able to inhale properly or a fear of suffocating, and a dry, harsh, croupy cough. As in the *Aconite* (*see* page 42) symptom picture, the child was caught out in a cold, dry wind. The cough can sound like a pine log being sawed. Strangely, a little snack or a warm drink helps to ease the symptoms.

- Another indication for *Spongia* would be where the sick person has a minor cold, burning, dry, sore throat and great hoarseness. The larynx is painful and worse for touch, and there is a constant desire to clear the throat. Sucking anything sweet increases the throat pain although eating and drinking can help the cough. The cough sounds dry, hollow or barking and comes from a spot deep in the chest.

User-friendly facts

For croup, remember to rotate a dose of *Aconite* (*see* page 42), then *Hepar sulph* (*see* page 69) and finally *Spongia* every 15 minutes initially and thereafter at longer intervals as the condition improves.

Better/worse facts	
Better:	**Worse:**
Eating warm food	Night before midnight
Drinking warm drinks	Warm room, after sleep
Bending forwards	Sweets
Lying flat	Cold, dry wind

Clinical facts
Cough, croup, laryngitis.

Danger facts
Severe shortness of breath and severe wheezing, with blue lips.

SYMPHYTUM (*Symphytum officinalis*)
Comfrey, Knitbone

Source facts
Tincture of the fresh root collected in autumn before flowering.
The fresh plant is also made into a tincture, which tincture is potentized.

Chat facts
This herb is the orthopaedic equivalent for bones as *Arnica* (*see* page 47) is for bruises. That is why it is commonly known as knitbone. The bruised leaf can be applied directly onto the sore limb. Comfrey contains allantoin, a substance that promotes cell replication and thus speeds up healing.

Key facts
- **Injuries to bones**, cartilage and periosteum (membrane that is very rich in blood vessels and nerves and covers the bone)
- Bone fractures
- Non-union of fractures
- Injuries to eye from knocks, blows
- Ulcers on skin and in stomach

Description facts
- It has an excellent effect on bones as it reduces pain and encourages speedy healing of fractures and sprains that have caused bruising of the periosteum lining all bones. It is also wonderful for injuries to cartilage.

- It has a specific effect on injuries to the eye socket and the eyeball and must be compared with *Ledum* (*see* page 79) and *Arnica* (*see* page 47).
- Because of its high content of soothing mucilage, a herbal tea made of *Symphytum* or comfrey is useful to treat ulcers and coughs.

> **Better/worse facts**
>
> These are not especially differentiating in this remedy.

User-friendly facts

This remedy can be used as an adjunct to speed up healing of all bone injuries after they have been professionally set.

Clinical facts

Backache from injury to spine or cartilage, black eye, bone fractures, injuries to eyes, ulcers.

Danger facts

All bone injuries must be X-rayed and set correctly.

URTICA URENS/URTICA DIOCA (*Urtica*)
Stinging nettle

Source facts

Potentized tincture of the whole plant picked just before flowering.
Urtica works well as a tea, tincture and potency.

Chat facts

This herb can be taken as nettle tea to reduce the toxins and uric acid produced by excessive exercise or the overconsumption of meat. The key to the remedy lies in its common name of 'stinging nettle' – it produces stinging, burning pain on contact as well as urticaria (an allergic reaction showing on the skin as an itchy, raised, red lump or weal). As you can see, the word 'urticaria' is derived from the plant's name.

Key facts
- **Urticaria** (hives), bee stings
- **Stinging**, burning pains
- **Burns**, applied locally in tincture and taken internally in potency form
- Effects of eating shellfish
- Promotes the production of breast milk

Description facts

- This is the irreplaceable and number one remedy for burns. Use it immediately – the sooner, the better. Use the tincture neat or slightly diluted and apply it straight onto the burn. Reapply it frequently or keep the burn covered by a wet compress of *Urtica* tincture. Remoisten the compress as it dries out. Use the remedy in potency too. The stinging pain improves quickly. If used in time, it will prevent blistering (if there is blistering, think of following the *Urtica* with *Cantharis*, see page 57). If sunburn itches and burns, it will respond best to *Urtica*.
- Urticaria can be caused by a number of allergic reactions. *Urtica* can relieve the itching, stinging and burning irritation of this complaint, whether it is caused by excessive exercise, hot baths or an allergic reaction to eating shellfish.

Better/worse facts	
Better:	Worse:
Warmth (sometimes)	Exercise and bathing

Clinical facts
Bee stings, burns, gout, ill effects of shellfish, insufficient breast milk, rheumatism, sunburn, urticaria.

Danger facts
See **Burns, Danger facts**, page 124

If, after eating shellfish, there is a tight chest or a very swollen tongue, take the sick person to hospital immediately.

PART THREE

AILMENTS

GET HELP IF...

Get immediate professional help or go to the hospital if any of the following occurs:

Backache with fever and bladder infection

Bleeding – heavy and without obvious cause

Blue lips

Breathing problems – difficult, severe wheezing

Bruising – severe and unexplained

Burns – severe or large, covering more than twice the size of the person's palm, with bad blistering; if burns involve the face, flexures, perineum or hands, or if they are circumferential (go around an arm or leg)

Chest pains

Concussion

Convulsions and epileptic fits

Delirium without fevers

Dehydration, especially where there is loss of fluids (for instance vomiting and diarrhoea) with a diminished fluid intake

Diarrhoea with persistent bleeding

Discharges from ears or nose that are bloody after head injury

Fever – persisting above 39.5 °C or accompanied by a severely stiff neck and inability to put the chin onto the chest

Headache – long-lasting and very severe

Red streaks extending from a wound or bite up the limb towards the swollen lymph glands

Sight lost or impaired

Stab wounds

Swelling – quick, intense and severe; affecting the mouth or throat especially

Talk – unable to or with difficulty

Unconsciousness – total or partial, especially following injury; severe headache or chest pain

Urine dark with pale or white stool, quantity severely diminished or bloody

Vomiting without nausea and uncontrollable, with blood that persists

Yellow skin or eyes

Instructions for remedy usage – do's and don'ts

The following simple rules will help you look after your homoeopathic remedies as they are very sensitive. Although they may look and taste the same, they are definitely not alike. It is very important to buy your remedies from a reputable homoeopathic pharmacy that have incorporated the most sophisticated, modern manufacturing protocols and procedures. Homoepathic medicines are made up of lactose pellets, globules or tablets, and are named according to their size.

- Do not touch the globules with your fingers more than is necessary. Shake out enough into the cap to cover its base and empty it into your mouth.
- Keep the remedies out of the heat and sunlight.
- Store it in a cool, dark place, away from strong odours.
- Keep it out of reach of children and pets – the remedies taste too nice! However, remember that the remedies are non-toxic even if a child were to swallow the entire contents of a bottle.
- Do not drink, eat, smoke or brush your teeth five minutes before or after a dose of the remedy.
- Do not use any products with a strong smell (particularly those containing camphor, such as Spirits of Camphor, Camphor Cream, Vicks products or Albas to rub or inhale, or Swedenbitters) while using homoeopathic remedies.
- Do not drink coffee (even decaffeinated coffee) or any cola drinks while on homoeopathic remedies.

How to administer remedies

We recommend that you purchase the remedies in the Materia Medica section of the book (*see* pages 41–107) and any others mentioned in the ailment section that suit your particular circumstances. As already mentioned, we have included a few extra remedies in this section that are specific to certain conditions at first-aid level. Store all remedies in a childproof, heat-resistant bag or box.

Important note It is impossible for children or adults to poison themselves even if they were to swallow the contents of the whole kit.

> **Size of the dose**
>
> In homoeopathy, a dose of remedy of whatever size is sufficient to stimulate the vital force and effect a change. A dose must be large enough to be absorbed into the body through the mouth's membranes.
>
> We recommend 6 globules, or 2 tablets or about 10 drops of liquid potency for adults and infacts alike. If necessary, globules can also be crushed between two teaspoons and dissolved in water for babies.

How often to repeat the dose

The word 'dose' refers to the number of times the medicine is taken. The dose should be repeated, but frequency depends on how severe the symptoms are and how well the sick person responds to the treatment. To elaborate:

In very serious conditions, repeat the dosage every five to 30 minutes. Repeat at longer intervals as the sick person and the symptoms improve, that is, every hour and then every two hours. If the sick person feels no change or not even a slight improvement after six doses, reassess the situation and the remedy.

In less serious situations, symptoms can be treated every one to four hours as necessary to achieve steady improvement.

If the symptom picture changes, you may have to change the remedy, but be careful of becoming too anxious and impatient, and thus changing the remedy too quickly.

Alternating remedies

It is preferable to give only one remedy, but sometimes you may wish to alternate remedies. When treating croup, for instance, you can alternate *Aconite*, *Spongia* and *Hepar sulph* every 15 minutes until there is some improvement. Then you can extend the times between doses to every 30 minutes, thereafter to every hour and eventually to every two to four hours. The symptoms might change to those of *Kali bich* (thick, yellow-green, stringy mucus accompanied by a metallic cough) as the disease or healing progresses. If so, you will have to change remedies. By this time the person you are treating will not be as acutely ill and you may wish to administer the *Kali bich* every four hours.

Although using a single remedy remains preferable in general homoeopathic terms, sometimes the symptom picture is too vague to be accurate and more than one remedy might be required. In spite of what you may read in some homoeopathic books about the incorrectness of using more than one remedy, we have, in all our years of experience, never found this to have adverse effects when treating acute illnesses. In fact, in some cases it can be of great benefit to use more than one remedy for acute or first-aid conditions. After an accident, for example, the sick person may be shaking from shock and require *Gelsemium*. Soft-tissue injury would require *Arnica*; any injury to the bone may need *Ruta*; and for damaged nerve tissue, you would have to administer *Hypericum*.

Similarly, it is possible to use a homoeopathic remedy at the same time as using a herbal remedy, for instance applying *Calendula* tincture on a wound as well as taking *Arnica* internally. With this in mind, we have included **Handy household and herbal hints** under each ailment.

Because we are realistic about your initial lack of homoeopathic expertise, we want to assure you that you can also take remedies at the same time as conventional medication, and still benefit from both.

An excellent alternative is to consult a professional homoeopath to treat difficult acute situations that go beyond the scope of *Homoeopathy for the home*.

Once the sick person is better, that is, once all the symptoms have disappeared and do not recur for a reasonable amount of time, discontinue treatment.

Case taking
How to set about treatment in the home
Always observe the **Danger facts** and realize when you might need professional homoeopathic help or help from a hospital. Also consider the following guidelines:
- First of all, observe, observe and observe again.
- For your convenience and confidence, write down the symptom picture as you observe it.
- Decide which of these symptoms are different from the normal pattern of the sick person, or, on the other hand, which symptoms are highly exaggerated forms of the sick person's 'normal' behaviour. You will often be guided by the **Better/worse facts** in the Materia Medica section. If you are lucky enough to discover a strange, rare and peculiar fact (*see* page 31), you can settle on the prescription. Remember that three strong, clear symptoms are all that are needed to match a similar remedy to the illness (to help you, we have emphasized the unequivocal symptoms in bold).
- Refer to the card summary (*see* pages 225–239) for specific ailments and read up the two or three leading remedies which best cover the symptoms you are treating.

- If there is no improvement within six hours, be prepared to reconsider your prescription. Remember that sometimes the improvement changes can be subtle and are often noticed by an improvement in mood and temperament before the physical changes can be seen. So don't be too hasty to change horses midstream. Conversely, 'do not indulge in much foolish waiting' (Kent).

In constitutional homoeopathy, case taking is a much more complex procedure, as you will have understood from the discussion on constitutional types (*see* page 36).

'The patient's own account of his sensibilities are usually the most reliable ... investigate events that caused or occasioned the disease ... ask for more precise details of the disease ... observe the patient and obtain information from the patient's relatives.'

SAMUEL HAHNEMANN

ANXIETY

see Emotional states, page 152

BITES AND STINGS

A bite is a wound made by a person, an insect or an animal, whereas a sting is an injury caused by introducing poison to the body, usually by insects like bees and wasps, but also by plants like *Urtica* or stinging nettles (*see* page 106). Do your best to prevent tick bites that can cause tick bite fever. Bites by venomous snakes and spiders, and stings by bluebottles at the sea, can also occur. Please get professional help for snakebites and take *Ledum* (*see* page 79) every five minutes en route to the doctor or hospital.

As prevention is better than cure, it would be wise to take a simple snakebite venom aspirator with you on all camping or outdoor trips. These are cheap and easily available from camping stores. It is common sense to wear correct and protective footwear while in the bush, and to tuck your trousers into your boots or socks to prevent tick bites.

> **Danger facts**
> - A professional person must treat snakebites immediately. You should try to identify the snake as this will help in assessing how venomous it is.
> - If the bite becomes infected, a red streak may begin to extend from the site as the infection spreads through the lymphatic system. This could be an indication of blood poisoning and professional help should be sought.

Apis

- Insect bites, especially bee stings
- Urticaria after insect bites – the body may be covered with large, elevated, white weals of urticaria (hives)
- Burning, stinging, prickling pain with shiny, rosy-red skin colour
- Much swelling after bites – it seems as if the skin will rip
- Parts of body are intolerant of heat and the slightest touch
- Better for cold applications
- Intense itching
- No thirst

Arnica
- Worse for the slightest touch
- Excessive bruising, more than you would expect from a bite

Ledum
- After insect and in particular mosquito bites
- The skin surrounding the bite is cold, pale, mottled and often very swollen
- Burning, stinging pains that are better for cold applications
- Appropriate for wounds that do not bleed
- Alternate with *Apis* if indicated

Silicea
- Promotes expulsion of foreign bodies from tissue, for example if sting remains in skin
- Skin looks unhealthy and every wound becomes infected and suppurates

Staphysagria
- Severe itching that is relieved by scratching, but the itching changes location while scratching
- Worse for touch
- Better for warmth
- Worse for cold

Urtica
- Itching skin with red, raised blotches and swelling (urticaria)
- Better for warmth and worse for cold applications

Handy household and herbal hints
Bites and stings
To repel insects:
- Eating a lot of garlic before a camping trip is reputed to keep insects (and everyone else) away!

> **Handy household and herbal hints – continued**
>
> **Bites and stings – continued**
>
> - Insects like mosquitoes and midges can be repelled by making an infusion of feverfew or rue, sponging the skin with the cooled lotion and allowing it to dry.
> - The oils of lavender, citronella and eucalyptus rubbed onto exposed body parts also act as a repellent.
> - To prevent fleabites, wash your clothing in water containing wormwood, also known as fleabane.
>
> **For treatment of insects bites:**
>
> - Dab damp salt or vinegar on the bites
> - Rub or bandage raw onion or garlic over a bee sting or wasp sting
> - Try using oatmeal or banana paste on tick bites after the tick has been removed
> - Dab on a lotion of witch hazel, which is a powerful antiseptic and astringent
> - Apply wet, rinsed plantain leaves to stings
> - Rub *Bulbinella* or *Aloe vera* gel from the plant straight onto the bite
> - Wormwood, rue or sage leaves, pulped or infused and then made into a compress, alleviate the pain caused by spider and scorpion bites, and jellyfish stings
> - Nettle stings can be treated by rubbing dock or plantain leaves onto the affected area (interestingly, nettle and dock always grow in the same locality)

BLEEDING

Bleeding can occur in various forms after an injury. Arterial bleeding is bright red and gushes, and must be treated as an emergency. Venous bleeding is darker in colour and more passive, while capillary bleeding tends to ooze continuously. Depending on the size of the blood vessel and its locality, always use common sense when treating bleeding.

> **Danger facts**
>
> - Bloody diarrhoea that persists.
> - Coughing up bright red blood.

> - Apply pressure and raise the bleeding part above the heart if possible. Use a clean cloth and hold it in place even if it gets soaked through. Put another clean cloth on top of the first. If the wound is still bleeding after 10 minutes, go to the hospital, but keep applying pressure while on the way there.
> - Blood spurting from a wound means that an artery has been cut – it will not stop bleeding on its own. **This is an emergency.** If alone, phone someone to drive you to hospital as you cannot drive and at the same time apply the pressure needed. Apply very firm pressure against the bone in the groin or armpit to attempt closing off the blood supply temporarily.
> - Use your fist or a rolled-up cloth and get to the hospital as soon as possible.
> - If there is any vaginal bleeding in pregnancy, contact your gynaecologist or midwife immediately.

Belladonna

- Sudden onset
- Usually red face and dilated pupils, eyes shine
- Blood red with clots, gushing, feels warm to the sick person
- Pulse full and throbbing
- No thirst or thirst for cold water
- Useful in nosebleeds and very heavy menstrual flow

Calendula

- Dab pure *Calendula* tincture on dry cotton wool and apply it with pressure to a wound to stop bleeding (styptic)
- Also give by mouth in 30ch potency and repeat every 15 minutes if necessary
- Pains excessive, out of proportion to injury
- Nausea

Ferrum phos

- The sick person flushes easily
- Pulse rapid and thready (very weak)
- Nervous, sensitive, neither anxious nor restless
- The sick person is pale, anaemic

- Nosebleeds
- Diarrhoea with blood in the stools

Ipecac
- Bright red, gushing, profuse bleeding with nausea
- Much saliva and clean tongue
- No thirst
- Pulse weak
- Cold sweat

Phosphorus
- Red or pale bleeding
- Nosebleeds or chronic small bleeds
- Persistent bleeding after tooth extraction
- Bleeding haemorrhoids (piles)
- Pulse rapid, weak and soft
- Wounds bleed a lot, even if small
- Swollen gums that bleed
- Desires ice cold water, but when it gets warm in the stomach it causes vomiting
- Fearful, wants company

Handy household and herbal hints

Bleeding

- A coagulant like *Calendula* or tobacco causes coagulation of the blood and so stops further bleeding.
- Cayenne pepper works externally as a styptic. Just sprinkle it on the wound.
- Cuts will sting initially if lemon juice is applied, but it quickly stops the bleeding.
- Nettle (*Urtica*) tincture or *Calendula* tincture, which should form part of your first-aid kit, will often stop bleeding rapidly. In the case of a nosebleed, wet a ball of cotton wool with one of the tinctures, and place it in the nostril. Repeat if the bleeding doesn't stop within a few minutes.
- Apply fresh yarrow leaves to the cut as this herb is an excellent coagulant.

Bleeding table						
		Belladonna	Calendula	Ferrum phos	Ipecac	Phosphorus
Colour	Red	+	-	+	+	+
	Dark	-	-	-	+	-
	Other	Clots	-	-	-	Pale
Gushing		+ +	-	-	+	-
Hot		+	-	-	-	-
Nausea		+	+	-	+ + +	+
Pulse		Full and throbbing	-	Rapid and thready	Weak	Full or weak
Mental		Anxiety Fear	-	Not anxious or restless		Wants company Fearful
General		No thirst or thirst for cold water	-	-	No thirst -	Thirst for ice-cold water
		-	-	-	Vomiting	Vomits when water gets warm in stomach
		Sudden onset, dilated pupils, eyes that shine Red face	Haemo static Pain excessive	Easy, gushing	Clean tongue, cold sweat	Small wounds bleed persistently
		-	Chilly	Not robust	-	

BOILS

A boil is a painful, inflammatory swelling of a hair follicle that forms an abscess. It starts as a small nodule surrounded by redness. The inflammation progresses and becomes pustular. It is usually tender and painful, and may be accompanied by a mild fever.

> **Danger facts**
> - Be careful with boils on the face.
> - Do not press or squeeze boils.
> - A red line running from the boil to a lymph gland is a sign to call for professional help.
> - Boils that fail to come to a head may need lancing.
> - Be wary of boils that present with a high fever.
> - It is a good idea to treat a boil as soon as possible to prevent it from becoming larger and more serious, and to reduce the pain. Remember to repeat the selected remedy every few hours.

Apis
- Carbuncles (boils with many heads) with burning, stinging pain
- Skin swollen with a white or rosy colour
- Better for cold applications and cold air

Arnica
- Small, frequent, recurrent boils in crops (the boils erupt and heal, but a new set of boils erupt again soon thereafter)
- Boils can be symmetrical on the body

Ars alb
- Carbuncles and boils that burn
- Pain better for warmth
- Thin discharge
- Very offensive discharge

Belladonna
- Rapid onset of dry, burning, hot, swollen, shining skin
- Pimples develop into scarlet-red boils and whitlows with redness and throbbing
- Discharge bloody with pus

Hepar sulph

- Boils are sometimes surrounded by little pustules, hypersensitive to the slightest touch or to cold air, with splinter-like pain in the boil and surrounding area
- The boils and the sick person are worse for uncovering or coldness
- Discharge can be bloody and offensive, resembles old cheese

Merc sol

- Boils are irregularly shaped, tend to spread and there can be pimples or vesicles around the main eruption
- Moist eruptions

Silicea

- *Silicea* has an unhealthy skin that will easily suppurate and turn into boils
- The boils are sensitive to pressure and touch, are better for warmth and often have stitching pain
- The boils frequently leave hard lumps under the skin on healing, which can recur as boils

---

Handy household and herbal hints
Boils

- Boils may be a result of mineral or vitamin deficiencies. It would be helpful to correct the diet – avoid fatty, greasy foods and increase your intake of fresh fruit and vegetables. Take vitamins and minerals, especially zinc and vitamin C.
- Apply tea tree oil externally when the boil is in its initial stages. *Calendula* tincture or *Echinacea* tincture, mildly diluted, can also be applied in compresses to the boil. Poultices can be effective too – use any of the following: powdered golden seal, burdock root, kaolin, potato or raw onion, which are all are reputed to be helpful in drawing out the pus.
- Burdock tincture or *Echinacea* tincture can be taken every two to four hours in a dosage of 15 drops diluted in water.

BURNS

Most burns occur in the home and can be treated there if the burn has caused a red and painful skin but there is no blistering or oozing. Burns are caused by the sun, fires, scalds, chemical substances and electrical appliances. Cool the burnt area with cold water, ice or even alcohol if the skin is not broken and cover the burnt area loosely with dry gauze. Don't apply butter or oil to the skin or pop any blisters.

> **Danger facts**
> - Seek immediate help from a hospital if the burns are severe or large, covering more than twice the size of the person's palm, if the burns have blistered, are on the face, flexures, perineum or hands, or if the burns are circumferential (going around an arm or leg). Always remember to treat the burnt person for shock in addition to the burn. *Aconite* or *Gelsemium* is helpful for shock.
> - In severe burns, do not attempt to pull off clothing stuck to the wound.
> - If it is a large burn, immerse the dressed person in cold water.

Aconite
- Burns, sunstroke, sunburn
- Skin red, hot, swollen, dry and shiny with burning pains
- Better for fresh, open air
- Restlessness and anxiety

Cantharis
- For burns, scalds, sunburn
- Burns that blister, exposing raw skin with intense, burning pains
- Burning sensation of the skin before blister formation (small vesicles which coalesce to form larger blisters)
- Sudden onset of symptoms with rapid progression
- Extensive burns
- Better for cold applications
- Reduces the severe pain following a burn and helps to promote healing

Urtica

- This is the first remedy to think of for treating all minor burns. Keep this remedy in the kitchen for cooking burns
- Burns, especially mild, superficial burns
- May be used topically (straight onto the skin or slightly diluted) as tincture and at the same time be taken internally as potency
- Intense, burning, itching, stinging pains
- Better for warmth (opposite of *Apis*, *see* page 45), worse for touch
- Worse for cool, cold air and cold applications

Handy household and herbal hints

Burns

- Seek professional treatment if the burn is larger than the size of the affected person's palm and if there is blistering. The following suggestions are for first-degree burns covering a small area only, in which the skin surface is painful and red.
- Burns dehydrate the body very quickly so the burnt person should drink water, juice or honey and lemon in water frequently. A pinch of cayenne pepper in the water will help against shock.
- Potato, peeled and grated and put on the burned area, will be soothing.
- Sour fig leaves can be pulped and applied to the area. Keep in place with a crepe bandage.
- Vitamin E, pressed from the capsule onto the burnt skin is soothing.
- Apply *Aloe vera* gel or the juice of a *Bulbinella* plant to soothe the burnt area.
- *Urtica* (nettle) tincture or juice will take the sting out of a burn.
- Lavender oil prevents scarring.

CATARRH
see Sinusitis and catarrh, page 186

CHICKENPOX
see Children's infectious diseases, page 127

CHILDREN'S AILMENTS

TEETHING

Teething in infants can cause painful gums and be accompanied by earache, diarrhoea and mood changes. Some babies find the effort of pushing out teeth very stressful, while for others it is quite easy.

> **Danger facts**
> - Nothing significant.

Belladonna
- The child has a dry mouth with red, swollen and hot gums that are worse from cold and cold applications
- The eyes are bright and shiny with dilated pupils and the face may be red
- The teething can induce a fever with irregular peaks and restless sleep, during which the child may jerk awake, with talking and groaning
- Hot perspiration (on covered parts) accompanies the fever
- The teething pains come and go suddenly

Chamomilla
- The child behaves like a brat, is moody, hateful, inconsolable and beside himself
- Any child needing *Chamomilla* is angry and capricious – he demands an object and then throws it down or at you
- The pain is out of proportion to the condition, but he is better from being carried or driven around in a car
- The child may have teething diarrhoea, which resembles chopped egg and spinach and smells of rotten eggs, or a green, watery diarrhoea
- As in *Chamomilla* fevers, one cheek is red and hot, while the other is pale and cold

Nux vom
- The teething child is extremely irritable, worse for any reprimand and easily angered
- He is worse on waking and may wake up from sleep at about 3–4 a.m.
- The teething can be accompanied by a runny nose, sneezing and often constipation

Pulsatilla

- The teething child is weepy and clingy, with a changeable mood and stool
- The child is better from being carried around in fresh air
- The sore teeth and gums are better from cold compresses and ice-cold teething rings
- He refuses to drink even though his mouth is dry

Handy household and herbal hints

Teething

- If your child is having problems with teething, chamomile tea will bring some relief. Other herbal teas that alleviate the stress and irritation caused to the body include a tea made from liquorice or lemon balm.
- *Echinacea* will help prevent other infections like viral colds from developing.
- Chewing on ice-cold teething rings will also alleviate the pain.
- Diluted cloves on the gums can reduce pain.

CHILDREN'S INFECTIOUS DISEASES

The following discussion on the treatment of children's infectious ailments is given as a general guide and should be used for mild infections. Use your common sense and obtain professional advice if necessary. With so many children receiving vaccinations nowadays, the attacks of measles, mumps and German measles (rubella) that may occur in epidemics in schools, are often paradoxical – the expected symptoms are often different from the usual pattern of the illness and present with unusual rashes and symptoms. Again, when in doubt, consult a professional homoeopath.

CHICKENPOX

Chickenpox is a contagious disease with skin eruptions that start as little water-filled and very itchy blisters. As the blisters get older, they dry up into crusts while others are still erupting. The child is most infectious the day before any of the blisters erupt.

Danger fact

- Don't give the child anything containing aspirin.

Rhus tox
- Intense itching, with an eruption of water blisters, which feels better for warmth
- Think of this remedy first for treating chickenpox – it will help most cases by reducing the itching and speeding up the healing while the disease runs its course

Urtica
- Use the tincture or cream on the spots to reduce itching

GERMAN MEASLES (*Rubella*)
An infectious disease accompanied by fever, swollen lymph glands behind the base of the skull and a fine, itchy rash that starts in the face and spreads downwards. This disease can incubate for two to three weeks and is mild in children. Women who are in the first three months of pregnancy, must avoid catching this illness as it can damage the growing foetus.

Belladonna
- Fine, bright red rash, with fever
- Early stages of inflammation
- Red, flushed face
- Hot, dry, red skin and mucous membranes
- Shiny eyes with dilated pupils, sensitivity to light (photophobia)
- Hot head with cold limbs

Merc sol
- Swollen lymph glands often starting at the base of the skull
- Feels hot one minute and cold the next
- With sweating that does not alleviate the symptoms

Sulphur
- Red, itchy rash that feels worse for the warmth of a bed or a warm bath
- Appetite diminished, but there is an increased thirst for room temperature drinks
- Desires sweets
- A useful remedy at the end of an infection to clear up residual coughs and mucus

> **Danger fact**
> - Nothing significant.

MEASLES

The treatment of measles should be left to a professional homoeopath as this illness can become quite serious and will require expert advice. This acute and highly infectious disease has an incubation period of about 10 days and is transmitted by droplets spreading from the nose or throat. The early stage starts with a runny nose, eye inflammation (conjunctivitis), a cough and a faint rash. This often responds to *Euphrasia* or *Pulsatilla*. The really intense rash starts after four days and develops behind the ears and on the forehead, and spreads down to the feet. It is accompanied by a high fever (*see* Fever, page 162) and the skin will peel as the rash disappears. If the sick child does not respond, seek professional help.

> **Danger fact**
> - If the cough is very severe, the child has diarrhoea or an intense headache, seek professional help.

Euphrasia
- Inflamed, sensitive eyes
- Profuse and bland discharge from nose
- Cough better for lying down
- Better from rest in bed

Pulsatilla
- No thirst
- Chilly but desires fresh air
- Profuse, thick, yellow discharge from eyes
- Red rash, itching worse for warmth

MUMPS

Mumps is a viral infection of the salivary glands on one or both sides. The best diagnostic hint is that the child looks like a hamster. Orange juice or acidic drinks increase the pain immensely.

> **Danger fact**
> - The mumps virus can in some instances spread to other glands in the body, particularly the testicles. In adult males this is potentially serious.

Merc sol
- Swollen glands in the neck are very painful and often worse at night
- The sick person feels shivery, perspires heavily and is thirsty, but drinking liquids hurts her swollen glands
- Bad breath with a sore throat

Pulsatilla
- The pain in the swollen glands is erratic and variable
- The sick person feels weepy, wants sympathy and consolation
- No thirst
- Swollen glands are accompanied by thick, yellow, bland mucus
- If the pain spreads to the testicles (*see* Danger facts), this is a very useful remedy

Sulphur
- Swollen glands burn with pain
- Face and lips are red
- The sick person feels very sleepy
- More thirsty than hungry, but wants sweet drinks and foods
- Feels hot and wants to uncover herself

> **Handy household and herbal hints**
>
> **Children's infectious diseases**
>
> - Always keep a child warm, especially in winter when the night-time temperature drops and the bedroom can become very cold. During winter, an oil-filled heater on low often prevents the cold of a restless child, who has kicked off his bedding, from becoming a more severe chest infection.
> - Cut a child's fingernails short to stop secondary infections, which could develop from scratching himself.
> - Do not force a sick child to eat if he goes off his food, but offer him small quantities of soups and fruit juice frequently.
> - In the case of mumps, encourage an older child to eat chewing gum as this promotes saliva production and reduces the swelling of the parotid and salivary glands.
> - Herbal teas like chamomile, peppermint, elderflower and catnip are very pleasant (especially with a little honey) and will help reduce fevers and calm down irritability caused by not 'feeling well'.
> - Because of vaccinations, children rarely get measles or they get stranger versions of the viral infection. If there is eye and light sensitivity, keep him away from bright lights and television.

COLDS AND FLU

Influenza (flu) is a viral disease that changes and mutates annually. Homoeopathically, flu is dealt with by treating the individual's symptom picture that he produces, and not by fighting the specific virus of the moment. Thus you need to watch and assess the symptoms that the flu will produce.

Flu has many stages and can often be nipped in the bud, but if it does set in, you can shorten its duration and make it far less miserable. Sufficient bed rest, sleep, a sensible diet and taking in enough fluids will also aid recovery.

To build up your resistance against flu, consider taking *Influenzinum* 6ch, 7ch or 9ch. once a week, and every four hours at the very onset of the flu. Take the indicated remedy as soon as possible too.

> **Danger fact**
> - Nothing significant.
> - Secondary infections.

Aconite
- Chill after cold, dry winds, starts within a few hours of exposure
- Hot, burning face and glazed eyes
- Restless and anxious
- If given early, may prevent the attack

Allium cepa
- Acrid nasal discharge, with a bland discharge or watering from the eyes (opposite of *Euphrasia*, *see* page 64)
- Laryngeal symptoms with tickling in the voice box
- Colds from damp, cold weather
- Eyes red and burning, suffused and bloodshot with smarting tears
- Sensitivity to light (photophobia)
- Hacking cough, worse from inhaling cold air
- Catarrhal headache
- Worse from warm room and in the evening, better in open air

Arnica
- Sore, bruised, lame feeling as if beaten, and the bed feels too hard
- Wants to be left alone, says nothing is wrong with him, confused
- Hot head, cold body and red face
- Thirsty and restless
- Violent, spasmodic cough
- Nosebleed (compare *Ferrum phos*, *see* page 65, with its tendency to nosebleeds with colds)

Ars alb
- Restlessness and weakness out of proportion to the illness
- Sudden onset

- Very thirsty for sips of warm liquid
- Chilly and can't get warm, worse from cold and wet weather, and better from warm drinks, food and warm applications
- Must sit up to cough, frothy expectoration
- Burning discharges and watery colds
- Pale with a cold sweat
- Irritable, exacting and fastidious, for example wants all the pictures straightened
- Fearful, wants company
- Worse from midnight to 3 a.m.

Bryonia
- Slow onset of cold or flu
- Thirst for large quantities of liquid
- Dry mucous membranes and dry, parched lips
- Aching or stitching pains in back, head, eyes or limbs
- Worse for any motion (even for being carried if the sick person is a child), or even for breathing or moving the eyes
- Wants pressure on the painful part and wants to lie on it
- Dry cough
- Wants to be left alone

Eupator perf *(Eupatorium perfoliatum)*
- This is a very useful remedy for flu. It works well at a 6ch potency or even as a herbal tincture. Take every two hours for relief
- Violent, aching, bone-breaking pains, especially in arms and wrists, aching muscles
- Soreness of skin at onset of flu
- Intense backache
- Restless, chilly, weakness with dizziness (vertigo) and nausea
- Sore, throbbing headache, worse in back of head, aching eyeballs
- Bilious headache
- Painful cough from laryngeal tickle, must hold chest
- Hoarseness in morning
- Raw, hot, sore chest and bronchi, worse at night
- Thirsty, but drinking causes vomiting
- Better for perspiration, except for the headache

Ferrum phos
- Onset of flu
- Flushed cheeks
- Hard, dry cough
- Soft pulse

Gelsemium
- Slow onset of flu
- Aching body, heavy limbs and chills up and down the back
- Headaches in the back of the head with stiffness in the neck
- Flushed face with drooping eyelids
- Dull, confused, drowsy, trembling and weak
- No thirst
- Dry cough
- Watery, burning nasal discharges
- Better for movement, stimulants, urination
- Worse at 10 a.m., in damp, cold weather or after a warm spell in winter

Hepar sulph
- Chilly, hypersensitive, irritable and touchy
- Worse from dry, cold winds and draughts
- Perspires easily and offensively
- Desires sour things and warm drinks
- Coughing when the sick person gets cold or is uncovered
- Croupy cough improved by steam

Kali bich
- Flu and colds from exposure to hot weather or cold damp
- Wandering pains (throughout the body)
- Pain at bridge or root of nose
- Stringy, yellow-green, tough, lumpy or thick discharges
- Blocked nose with watery, profuse nasal discharge
- Postnasal drip
- Sinusitis with fullness at root of nose
- Throat dry and burning, often with hoarseness, laryngitis

- Worse from 2–4 a.m.
- Brassy cough

Nat mur
- Colds and flu after grief
- Thick, white or clear, watery, acrid discharges
- Easily angered, worse for consolation or fuss
- Hammering headaches
- Sneezing early in the morning
- Alternate fluid and dry colds
- Cold sores around lips
- Feels weak on waking
- Face pale, greasy
- Dry spot in throat causes tickle and brings about coughing
- Thirst for large quantities of liquid
- Worse from 9–11 a.m.
- Better from open air and sweating

Nux vom
- Angry, impatient, irritable and can't stand pain
- Rawness in throat and larynx
- Nose blocked, but water runs from it, blocked at night
- Violent sneezing and coughing
- Lumbar backache, must sit up to turn over
- Easily chilled, stays covered
- Coughing causes nosebleeds
- Worse early in the morning
- Worse from cold, dry, open air, winds and draughts
- Desires warm drinks and is very hungry
- Feels better after sleeping

Pulsatilla
- Better from cold, fresh, open air, erect posture or sitting up, gentle movement
- Worse from getting feet wet, from warmth and in the evenings
- No thirst

- Chilly but desires fresh air and open windows
- Emotional and weepy
- Profuse, thick, bland yellow or green discharges
- Nausea aggravated by fatty foods
- Changeable symptoms
- Pale face

Rhus tox
- Restless, aching flu with soreness and stiffness in the muscles and joints
- Pain is worse lying still in bed or on first moving, but feels better after loosening up
- Pain is helped by a warm bath and rubbing
- Chilly and better for warmth
- Urticaria with high fever
- Desire for cold milk
- Tongue coated, with a triangular, red tip
- Sore throat with swollen glands, better for warm drinks
- Flu and colds from cold, damp weather or getting wet
- Laryngitis from air conditioning or cold winds
- Tickling behind the upper sternum causes a dry, hoarse, tearing cough
- Red, swollen nose dripping water and sneezing

Handy household and herbal hints

Colds and flu

- Garlic in the form of a cut-up clove hidden in a teaspoon of honey or as capsules should be taken every few hours as it acts as an antiseptic to all the catarrh and stops it from becoming gluey and very thick.
- *Echinacea* tincture is antiviral and helpful. Take 15 drops in water every two to four hours.
- Propolis, a substance derived from queen bees, can be very helpful.
- Make a herbal tea by using some of the following dry or fresh herbs – elder-berry flowers, peppermint, yarrow, boneset, sage, vervain or ginger root. Use one tablespoon of each of the herbs chosen in two litres of water, let it steep for 10 minutes and sweeten with a little honey. Drink as much as you like.

> - Flu is caused by a variety of viruses, and the infection is spread by droplets in coughs and sneezes. Bed rest and lots of fluids usually help – honey and lemon juice can be taken every hour and extra vitamin C.

COLIC
see Cramps and Colic, page 142

CONJUNCTIVITIS
see Eye infections, page 157

COUGHS
Coughs often accompany viral infections. They are the body's attempt to expel mucus generated in the upper respiratory tract, that is, in the nose, throat or bronchial tubes. As such it is never a good idea to merely suppress the cough. The correctly chosen remedy should help the body to get rid of the underlying infection, clearing away the mucus and relieving the cough. If you have no response, the sick person's mood deteriorates or her energy becomes depleted, seek professional homoeopathic help. In children with recurrent or 'nursery school' colds and coughs, professional constitutional treatment will help to strengthen the child's immune system.

> **Danger facts**
> - Obtain help if there is severe difficulty with breathing, severe wheezing and chest pain, shortness of breath, if the breathing is much faster than normal, and if the sick person has difficulty talking.
> - You should also get immediate professional help if there is a sudden, severely sore throat, constriction, a high fever with an inability to swallow, great drooling and a reluctance to open the mouth, a blue tinge to the mouth and difficulty inhaling.
> - Prolonged coughing must be screened for tuberculosis.
> - If the croup is so severe as to impede breathing, or with bluish discoloration of the lips, take the child to the nearest hospital or emergency room.
> - Cough with blood or blood streaked expectoration

Aconite
- Dry, violent, croupy cough
- Cough caused by exposure to dry, cold winds
- Cough accompanied by anxiety and fear
- Worse at midnight
- For the initial onset of croup, caused by exposure to cold air

Ars alb
- Burning in chest or feeling of smoke in lungs, with a fear of suffocating
- Tight, dry or wheezy cough
- Worse from midnight to 3 a.m.
- Chilly, thirsty for sips
- Better for sitting upright or raising head

Belladonna
- Sudden, dry, barking or short, tickling cough
- Cough with sore throat or hoarseness
- Red face with coughing

Bryonia
- Dry, hard, painful cough
- Holds chest and sides while coughing
- Stitching pains with every breath or cough
- Pain behind breastbone caused by the movement of coughing
- Severe headache with coughing
- Must sit up to cough even though the sick person feels worse for movement
- Cough worse for any motion, even deep breathing, and warm rooms
- Great thirst for large quantities of liquid
- Wants to rest and lie on the painful area

Drosera (*Drosera rotundifolia*)
- Continuous bouts of dry, barking cough, paroxysmal
- Cough worse lying down
- Cough worse for talking, eating or drinking

- Cough worse from midnight to 2 a.m.
- Holds onto the chest while coughing
- Useful in viral whooping cough epidemics

Euphrasia
- Dry, hard cough that is better for lying down
- Burning secretion of tears and bland, running nose may present

Ferrum phos
- Dry, hacking cough with some blood in the expectoration
- Worse from being exposed to cold air and after eating

Hepar sulph
- Cough from exposure to cold winds
- Coughing starts when the sick person gets cold, even if only a part of the body is chilled (even putting a finger out from under the covers will set off a coughing fit)
- Croupy cough, better for steam
- Cough better if the sick person bends her head back
- Hoarseness and laryngeal cough
- Cough can also be catarrhal
- Profuse sweating with coughing
- Loose, rattling, choking cough

Ipecac
- Cough with nausea, wheezing
- Can present together with a tendency to vomit or gag, or with paroxysms of retching, accompanied by a blue/red face
- Incessant, suffocating cough
- Whooping cough with loose, coarse rattles in chest without expectoration
- Constriction and tightness of chest
- Salivates excessively with cough, but tongue is clean
- Coughing causes nosebleeds
- Moist asthma, mucus bubbly
- Breathing rapidly becomes difficult

Kali bich
- Cough with thick, sticky or stringy, yellow-green mucus
- Cough from postnasal drip or sinusitis
- Hoarse voice
- Pain in ears with cough
- Pain in throat when sticking out the tongue
- Croupy, metallic-ringing cough

Merc sol
- Watery, yellow or green mucus, often with a sore throat and profuse sweating that does not help the situation
- Alternately hot and cold

Phosphorus
- Colds go to chest
- Tickling or hacking cough with tightness
- Painful cough with burning in chest behind breastbone
- Oppression of chest, feels like a weight on the chest
- Rapid, difficult breathing, wheezing
- Must sit up with cough, cough is worse for lying down or lying on the left side
- Dry cough becomes loose and fruity with yellow-green mucus, from chest or nose; mucus can taste sweet or salty
- Hard, wheezing, dry, violent and painful hacking, exhausting, with retching
- Burning in air passages
- Cough is worse at night, and from the change from warm temperature to cold, from talking, and is often accompanied by hoarseness
- Taking in liquids can help cough

Pulsatilla
- Cough worse in a warm room, during warm weather
- Cough better for open air
- Cough loose during daytime and dry at night
- Dry mouth and no thirst
- Must sit up to cough
- Thick white, yellow or green mucus from chest or nose

Spongia
- Hacking, harsh, deep, hollow, barking, dry, croupy coughs
- Larynx constricted and burning
- Croup worse for inhaling and before midnight
- Anxiety of suffocation and difficult, wheezing breathing
- Wakes around midnight to 4 a.m.
- Coughs from talking and dry, cold winds
- Cough improved by drinking warm liquids or eating
- Hoarseness with coughs, colds and laryngitis
- Difficult breathing, better for bending forward

Handy household and herbal hints
Coughs
- Clear the mucus from the nose and chest frequently (teach a child how to blow her nose one nostril at a time).
- Encourage postural drainage by letting the individual lie with her head lower than her waist. Cup your hands and beat firmly on her back for up to 10 minutes and repeat this a few times a day. This enables her to cough up the mucus more easily.
- Drink plenty of fluids and inhale steam.
- Avoid dairy products, sugar, white bread and junk food which increase mucus.
- Avoid food and drinks that use sulphur dioxide as a preservative. Bananas can constrict the chest in asthmatic children, so don't give them bananas while they are coughing.
- Avoid tobacco fumes at all costs.
- Lemon and honey, added to a cup of thyme tea (one teaspoon of dried thyme to a cup of boiling water), soothes and aids expectoration.
- The addition of garlic and onions to the diet makes the mucus more liquid and easier to expectorate.
- Make a tea with a combination of some of the following herbs – ginger, basil, cinnamon, cardamom, elecampane, coltsfoot, thyme, liquorice, comfrey, lemon balm or horehound. Use one teaspoon of each herb chosen in two litres of water. Simmer for 10 minutes and add honey for taste and sweetness.

CRAMPS AND COLIC

In true colic the pains are very sharp and can cause the sick person to double up in pain. The pain can be severe enough to cause vomiting. The abdomen is not hard or distended. You can often hear the gurgling sounds of gas that, if it can be expelled, will make the sick person feel better.

> **Danger facts**
> - Get professional help immediately if the pain is severe, recent and with abdominal distension and hardness, very tender to pressure, if there is nausea or vomiting, or if the stools contain blood or have a tarry colour.
> - Severe abdominal pain lasting several hours after previously good health also needs immediate professional attention.

Carbo veg
- The simplest food disagrees with the sick person and can cause abdominal distress and colic
- Excessive accumulation of gas in stomach and intestines, leading to flatulent colic
- Cannot bear tight clothing around waist and abdomen
- The upper part of the abdomen can be greatly distended
- The pains are better from passing wind (upwards or downwards)
- The flatus can be very offensive
- The colic and wind pains force the sick person to double up
- Griping and cramping pains in the abdomen, forcing the sick person to double up, 30 minutes after eating

Colocynthis
- The sufferer doubles up from the pain and writhes in agony
- The pain is better for strong pressure on the painful spot, for instance lying on the abdomen to relieve abdominal pain. Warmth can also bring some relief, as can lying doubled up (pulling the legs up to the chest). The pains can be focused around the belly button
- Worse after eating or drinking, and the sick person may develop nausea, vomiting and diarrhoea from the pain

- Restlessness, twisting and turning to obtain relief
- Intestines feel as if squeezed between stones
- Violent, cutting, griping, grasping, clutching or radiating colicky pains (mostly around the belly button) that come in waves. There is a constricting sensation as though a metal band were being tightened around the cramping part
- The sick person feels irritable and extremely angry – the cramping can also be brought on by anger, indignation, humiliation and grief
- Restlessness or faintness and weakness

Mag phos
- The most general antispasmodic remedy
- Sudden, intolerable, severe, spasmodic pains that can be erratic or lightning-like
- There is distension and bloating that are not improved by passing flatus
- Abdominal cramps and colic that is better from warmth, extremely hot applications, hot drinks, hot baths and hot-water bottles; also better from pressure, bending, rubbing; generally worse from cold
- Flatulent colic, must loosen clothing
- Useful for menstrual cramps

Nux vom
- Flatulent distension and spasmodic colic
- There may be a strong desire to pass a stool, but the sick person cannot pass anything of note
- He feels that vomiting may make him feel better but cannot vomit
- Irritable, easily angered, short-tempered and fault-finding
- The pains are severe, cutting and griping, with a bruised sensation of the stomach muscles
- This remedy is especially useful for cramps caused by constipation
- The pains are worse from eating and drinking, motion (pain at every step), cold and anger, and are better from rest, heat and short naps

> **Handy household and herbal hints**
>
> **Cramps and colic**
>
> Do not ignore abdominal pain as it can be a danger signal. Pain can be caused by dietary indiscretions, food poisoning, tension, which can cause a 'spastic colon', bladder infections, period pain, and so on.
>
> - A hot-water bottle wrapped in a towel can soothe the area of pain. Chamomile tea, taken often with a little ginger powder added to it, will relieve spasms.
> - Peppermint tea and honey to which some aniseed or cinnamon has been added can be helpful. Sip this frequently.
> - Thyme tea is mildly antispasmodic and acts as an antiseptic to gas-producing bacteria in the intestines.
> - Catmint tea reduces fever, calms the nervous system, reduces stomach cramps, expels flatulence and prevents diarrhoea.
> - Slices of fresh ginger in hot water or even dried ginger from your spice rack will help break the colic pains and help expel gas.
> - Caraway seeds are traditionally added to cabbage to stop it from causing undue gas and to help the body expel the gas.

DENTAL PROBLEMS

see Mouth ulcers and dental problems, page 181

DEPRESSION

see Emotional states, page 152

DIARRHOEA

Diarrhoea is the passing of frequent stools that are usually loose and watery. This loss of body fluids can lead to the loss of vital vitamins and minerals, leaving the sick person tired, exhausted and debilitated. Diarrhoea can be both an acute and a chronic condition. In *Homoeopathy for the home*, we help you to treat acute episodes of diarrhoea.

> **Danger facts**
> - The signs of dehydration are a dry mouth, sunken eyes, depressed fontanelle in babies and diminished skin tone – the skin can easily be pinched upwards.
> - If there are signs of dehydration and the person cannot keep the rehydration fluid down because it causes vomiting, seek professional help.
> - Children are much more susceptible to dehydration, so err on the side of caution.

Ars alb
- Diarrhoea often occurs at the same time as vomiting, and can start at midnight and last until 2 a.m. or 3 a.m.
- Intense weakness, exhaustion and collapse
- Restlessness, anxiety and worry
- Nausea, retching and vomiting immediately after eating or drinking
- Cutting pains in the abdomen before, during and after diarrhoea
- Diarrhoea is watery, burning, acrid and foul (smells like putrefying meat)
- Sick person is very chilly and better from heat
- Thirsty for small sips of liquid (preferably warm)
- This is very useful for the classical picture of food poisoning (*see* page 165)

Chamomilla
- Irritability and intolerance of pain
- Foul, hot, green, watery, slimy, smelly stools with colic
- There may be chopped, yellow or white mucus, often with teething or undigested food in the stool. It can look like chopped spinach with scrambled eggs
- Hot and thirsty, hot sweat accompanies the pain

Merc sol
- Constant desire to pass a stool, but scanty stools are passed with much painful, ineffectual straining and a sensation of not having evacuated completely
- The stools are green, slimy and foul
- There can be cutting, colicky pain and nausea, and the stools are sometimes preceded by chilliness and vomiting
- Diarrhoea can be worse at night

- Intense thirst
- Foul breath with swollen, coated tongue
- Offensive perspiration

Nux vom
- Diarrhoea from excess alcohol and rich foods
- Sick person is irritable
- Stools frequent; small evacuations with much urging and a constant desire to pass small amounts of stool
- A constant sense of unease in the rectum
- Abdominal cramps

Phosphorus
- Painless, copious, debilitating diarrhoea
- Fetid stools and flatus
- The watery stools pour out and can be involuntary; they contain undigested food and lumps of white mucus
- Burning in the rectum and anus
- Great weakness after passing a stool, with diarrhoea increasing in the morning

Podophyllum
- Gastroenteritis, colicky pain and bilious vomiting
- Diarrhoea preceded by heat and colicky pain in abdomen
- The stools are profuse, fetid, gushing and preceded by gurgling and rumbling in the abdomen. They are often yellow or green, watery, and contain undigested food and mucus
- Diarrhoea is painless and followed by weakness
- There is often a loose stool immediately after eating or drinking
- Worse from 3– 9 a.m., from motion and in hot weather
- Diarrhoea with teething in babies, or diarrhoea after eating fruit and drinking milk
- Involuntary stool with flatus
- Hot, flushed cheeks with the diarrhoea
- Fidgety and restless, can't sit still

Pulsatilla

- Diarrhoea with or after menstruation or after taking in fruit, cold food and drink, ice cream and rich foods
- No two stools are alike
- The diarrhoea is often preceded by colic and pain in the small of the back
- Frequent, ineffectual urging as if diarrhoea would occur
- No thirst and weepy

Sulphur

- Early morning diarrhoea that drives the sick person out of bed, especially at 5 a.m.
- The anus is very red
- The stools are foul, watery, greyish, slimy, frothy, fetid and painless while passing, but leave a feeling of pressure and burning in the rectum after a stool, and a lingering odour in the air

---

Handy household and herbal hints

Diarrhoea

Acute diarrhoea can be caused by viral gastroenteritis, eating too much fruit, food poisoning, dysentery, traveller's diarrhoea, and as a part of other acute illnesses.

- Avoid all foods that are difficult to digest and eat foods that are binding, for example white rice, mashed potatoes, grated apple and mashed banana.
- Cooked barley or barley water is an excellent diarrhoea aid for infants.
- Strong, black tea contains a lot of tannin and this can also bind the protein in the large intestine, reducing diarrhoea.
- Make a brewed tea using ginger root, peppermint, sour fig, cardamom, cinnamon, blackberry roots, raspberry leaf and agrimony leaves or flowers.

Digestive disorders, including food poisoning and vomiting

- For food poisoning (*see also* page 165), allow the body to eliminate the 'bad food' by vomiting it out or allowing the first couple of diarrhoea stools. Only if the toxins in the food eaten cause ongoing vomiting and severe weakness, do you need to start treating the condition.

> - Do not allow the sick person to become dehydrated. Let him sip some grape juice, ginger ale or a commercial rehydrating mixture.
> - Make a tea by taking one teaspoon each of herbs such as chamomile, mint, thyme, ginger, angelica, fenugreek, cinnamon, lavender or nutmeg. Place it in a large mug of boiling water and allow it to steep. It will settle the stomach, allay some nausea and vomiting, and reduce spasms and colic. Add a little honey for sweetness and to prevent excess weakness. Sip this tea freely.

EAR INFECTIONS

Infections of the middle ear often originate in the throat and spread via the Eustachian tube, which connects the middle ear to the throat or pharynx. If treated early, you can resolve many simple earaches with the aid of these remedies. This will prevent them from progressing into more serious conditions that will need the help of a professional homoeopath. For the remedy to be similar, it must match the symptoms and the stage of the infection. *Aconite* (*see* page 42), for example, will only be successful in the very early stages. *Belladonna* (*see* page 51) is another 'early' remedy.

> **Danger facts**
> - Earache with severe weakness, headache, stiff neck, loss of alertness.
> - Ear discharge (if there are no grommets).
> - Earaches that, even if mild, linger for more than a week.
> - Sudden decrease in hearing or prolonged, mild hearing loss.
> - Sensitivity and/or redness in the mastoid (bony portion) behind the ear.
> - Very severe earache with high fever.
> - Foreign bodies in ear.

Aconite
- First stage after exposure to dry, cold winds
- Bright red ears
- High fever
- Sharp pain

- Often holds ear and screams with pain
- Great sensitivity to noise
- One cheek red and the other one pale (compare *Chamomilla*, *see* page 60 and *Pulsatilla*, *see* page 93)
- Anxious, restless
- Burning thirst for cold water

Belladonna
- Sudden onset of burning fever with throbbing pain in the ear
- Pain leaves as suddenly as it starts, comes in waves
- Child will cry out, jerk and roll his head in sleep
- The outer ear and ear canal, which is easily visible, may be bright red
- The pain can extend from the ear to the neck, throat and face
- The pain is worse from any jarring motion and lying down
- Often starts in right ear, often at 3 p.m. or 3 a.m.
- Little or no thirst

Chamomilla
- Earache from teething
- Pain is severe and drives the sick person frantic
- Heat and swelling of the ear
- Redness of the cheek on the same side as the sore ear
- Ears feel blocked
- Bad temper, irritability, tantrums
- Desire to be held and carried
- Ears are sensitive to cold wind,, noise and are soothed by warmth

Ferrum phos
- The symptom picture is less intense than *Aconite* or *Belladonna*, but the sick person has a very definite sore ear
- Pale red flush alternating with marked pallor
- Deafness and noises in the ear
- This remedy should be repeated every 30 minutes in the early stages
- The earache is often accompanied by the early stages of a cold or sore throat

Hepar sulph

- Sensitive, sweaty and chilly
- Ears sensitive to touch, wind and cold air
- Ears feel better for wrapping the head or covering the ears
- Stitching pain
- Sore throat with pain extending to the ear on swallowing
- Tenderness in bone behind ear (mastoid)
- Sores and small, pustular boils in the ear canal
- Discharges from ear
- Irritability

Merc sol

- Earache worse for warmth, especially at night
- Pain worse at night
- Profuse, offensive perspiration and head sweats
- Salivation, enlarged flabby tongue, offensive breath
- Yellow-green discharge from the ear
- Pain in ears extends to teeth
- Earache accompanied by sore throat
- Boils in external ear canal
- Itching in ear
- Glands swollen beneath ear

Pulsatilla

- Changeable symptoms and moods
- Irritable, tearful, vulnerable, whiny and clingy
- Craves company, attention and consolation
- Discharges from ears and nose thick, yellow-green, bland
- No thirst
- Earache from getting feet wet, from or during colds
- Earache better for cool applications and worse in a warm room
- Earache worse at night
- Difficulty hearing with blocked ears
- Earache after mumps
- Better sitting up

- External ear is red
- Can hear better in a car

Silicea
- Chilly and worse for cold air and draughts
- Ear is worse for cold and moving around
- Likes to lie with head on hot-water bottle
- Pain worse from noise
- Tingling itching in Eustachian tube – sticks fingers in ears to relieve the sensation
- Blocked ears with hearing coming and going as ears 'pop' with yawning or swallowing
- Mastoid pain (bony part behind the ear)
- The left ear is often infected
- Useful when ear infections linger on

Handy household and herbal hints

Ear infections

- Cover a hot-water bottle with a towel and apply local heat to the side of the face.
- Mix two tablespoons of warm olive oil with two drops of clove, peppermint, mullein or tea tree oil. Drop the oil mixture into the ear with a dropper and put a large plug of cotton wool into the ear to protect the pillow and sheets from the oily substance.
- The most important antimicrobial herbs that boost the immune system are *Echinacea*, garlic, wild indigo and blue flag. Herbs that are anticatarrhal and reduce the amount of mucus produced by the membranes lining the entire upper respiratory tract are also very useful. Examples of these are garlic, elderflower and golden rod.
- Excess wax in the ear will dissolve if you put warm olive or almond oil in the ear for a few nights.

EMOTIONAL STATES

Homoeopathy can help to alleviate many emotional states and reactions. We don't expect you to be able to handle severe depression, anxiety or pathological mental states, for example manic depression. Neither can acute homoeopathic medication be expected to take the place of psychotherapy. However, with life's ups and downs, stresses and worries, we often find ourselves in emotional states with reactions that are difficult to handle. We have included this section to treat these transient emotional conditions and are confident that you will find it very useful. If the emotional conditions persist or where there is no response to these remedies, please seek professional homoeopathic help.

> **Danger facts**
> - If no improvement 48 hours after remedies, seek professional help.
> - Suicidal patients must be taken very seriously.

Aconite
- For the effects of fright
- Extreme anxiety and fear with restlessness
- Panic attacks with violent palpitations and shortness of breath
- Strong fear of death, even makes predictions about his death
- Claustrophobia, fear of crowds, flying
- Give after a shock, for example after a car accident

Argentum nit (*Argentum nitricum*)
- For anticipation, anxiety, panic attacks and fear
- The person needing *Argentum nit* becomes restless and talkative, and walks around hurriedly, fearing to be late
- To be taken before exams, and by the student who is anxious about not finishing within the allocated time and who jots down disorganized, chaotic thoughts. This student is so nervous and anxious that she can't think straight
- There are numerous fears – of heights, flying, looking up at tall buildings or driving
- May feel claustrophobic in lifts or shopping malls
- Fear, sometimes accompanied by diarrhoea

- A craving for sugar and chocolates, but this upsets her, causing diarrhoea, flatulence and heartburn

Arnica
- Effects of overwork and overexhaustion
- After shock, for example after accidents
- Will tell you that she doesn't need help when it is obvious that she does. She will refuse X-rays and so on, only to discover that her condition is much worse the next day

Ars alb
- Overwhelming anxiety with restlessness
- Panic attacks with trembling
- Needs company and reassurance
- Critical of others
- Fears to be alone, fear of illness and death
- Worse from midnight to 2 or 3 a.m.
- Perfectionist and fussy

Chamomilla
- Irritable, easily angered, moody and hateful
- Babies, especially in teething, cannot bear any pain. They are better if they are carried around or taken for drives in a car. They ask for things and then throw them
- For temper tantrums in children who are then inconsolable
- Adults in a *Chamomilla* state are nervous, easily angered, cannot tolerate anyone or anything and are hypersensitive to pain. They feel as if 'their nerves are on edge'

Colocynthis
- Ailments from anger or humiliation, causing cramps or spasms all over the system, for example colic, sciatica

Gelsemium
- For anticipation, anxiety, apprehension and stage fright
- For the person who becomes paralysed by fear, the student who goes blank during an examination and hands in an empty paper, or the performer who gets stage fright

- Take before tests, exams and interviews
- Take the remedy the day, night, and just before, the event
- Fear and trembling, legs feel as if they will turn to jelly, feels weak at the knees
- Diarrhoea and urgent urination from nerves
- Mental dullness or loss of memory from emotion or anticipation
- In a situation of anxiety, often wants to be held or given an alcoholic drink to steady the nerves
- May also be taken after fright or shock, bad news or excitement
- Think of taking *Gelsemium* after a car accident or near escape

Ignatia
- Sighing and yawning
- Ailments from grief, strain, disappointed love, suppression of emotions
- Hysterical outbursts
- Contradictory, paradoxical symptoms, changeable moods
- Physical ailments from emotional causes
- Likes to be alone to grieve silently
- Sympathy makes her feel worse
- Pain in small spots, feels like a nail driven in
- *Globus hystericus* (sensation of a lump in the throat)

Nat mur
- Grief and sadness
- Depression and moodiness
- Sadness, but may be unable to cry or cries alone
- Desires to be alone
- Unable to accept sympathy because it will make her feel worse or cry more
- Headaches and colds from grief
- Many symptoms are worse at 10 a.m.
- Craves salt or bitter foods from grief

Nux vom
- Irritability
- Craving for stimulants and food
- Premenstrual irritability and anger

- Hypersensitivity to noise, light, odours
- Insomnia from overwork and overstimulation
- Nervous and excitable
- Great anxiety
- Impatient, hurried feeling
- Because of the irritability, queues and traffic become too much and she exhibits 'road rage'

Pulsatilla
- Weepiness
- Crying easily and out of control
- Wants consolation and comfort
- Feels forsaken, vulnerable and alone
- Depression or sadness with weepiness
- Weepiness before periods

Silicea
- Profound dread of failure
- Afraid of things before they actually happen
- Low self-confidence, wants to give up before she starts something
- Convinced she will fail, but actually does quite well
- Exhausted after the event
- Perfomance anxiety causes her to dwell compulsively on small details
- Paralysed by anxiety or indecision
- Stage fright

Staphysagria
- For abusive situations where the sick person feels unable to fight back and consequently bottles up all her feelings. This happens until she can't take any more and then she explodes with rage, throwing breakable objects
- For ailments after abuse, emotional hurt and anger
- For feelings of being the underdog – 'it's not fair'
- A feeling of great injustice and a desire to take the perpetrator to court

Handy household and herbal hints
Emotional states
- There are many herbs that work on the mental, emotional and psychological spheres, as well as strengthening the nervous system.
- Take care of yourself, particularly during times of stress, follow the correct diet and lead a healthy lifestyle. Stress is ubiquitous and can be triggered by many things – work conditions, difficult relationships, the lack of a support structure and good friendships, poor health, reading bad news in the newspapers or seeing it on television, and even climatic effects.
- Adequate sleep and rest is vital as this allows the body to enter the 'rest and recuperation' mode essential for recovery from ill health and for the maintenance of normal body functions. At times of stress or illness, our sleep requirements are increased. Children and teenagers going through periods of fast physical growth also need extra sleep – up to 10 hours a day.
- In terms of diet, it is important to eat a sensible diet rich in fruit and vegetables and complex carbohydrates, with a small, daily amount of protein. Avoid foods that contain artificial colourants and flavourants as these take more of the body's energy to process, metabolize and excrete.
- Herbs that feed the nervous system include oats that can be taken as a tincture of *Avena sativa* (take 15 drops in a little water three times a day and another dose before bedtime to aid sleep). Otherwise have oats porridge daily.
- Other herbs that are nutritive to the nervous system include *Passiflora*, skullcap, St John's Wort, vervain, damiana herb and chamomile. They can all be taken as teas, or are available as tablets or tinctures.

Anxiety
- Lime blossom (*Tiliea*) makes a delicious smelling tea and is an effective herb for calming an anxious state of mind.
- Skullcap and valerian root are very effective as they stop you having anxious thoughts. Kava kava is calming and reputedly makes you feel as calm as if you were on holiday on a Polynesian island!
- Chamomile tea at night will often help children to sleep, as will massaging their feet with a few drops of lavender oil.

> **Anxiety – continued**
> - Although valerian root has a strong smell as a tea or tincture, it is also a pain-reliever in cases where the pain is associated with anxiety and tension. It also alleviates insomnia. Combine it with *Passiflora*, *Avena* or hops for insomnia. In tincture form, all these herbs can be taken in a dosage of 15 drops three times a day and again before bedtime to aid sleep.
>
> **Depression**
> - The basic underlying causes of depression must be treated, but certain herbs such as lavender, verbena and rosemary have a good reputation for lifting the spirits.
> - Taken internally, St John's Wort reduces anxiety and depression. It acts slowly and may need to be taken for at least a month before it takes effect.

EYE INFECTIONS

Eye infections affect the membrane covering the eye. The eye becomes sore, bloodshot and can water profusely. A dislike of bright lights (photophobia) may manifest.

There are many causes for inflamed eyes and these can range from viral or bacterial infections to allergies or irritations from foreign objects, even if they are no longer in the eyes. Allergies to smoke, the chemicals in swimming pools or pollen during the hay fever season can all cause redness, pain, itching, tearing and discharges.

> **Danger facts**
> - Please note that expert attention is necessary in all cases mentioned below.
> - Any suspicion of a foreign body in the eye needs instant, expert examination.
> - Chemicals (including household detergents and products) in the eye.
> - Very severe eye pain.
> - Any loss of vision.
> - Changes in the shape of the pupil.
> - Marked red line encircling the iris (the coloured portion of the eye).

AILMENTS

Aconite
- This is the '*Arnica*' of the eye
- This should be used after any foreign body has entered the eye, even an irritating speck of dust, as it removes the pain
- Sudden onset of watering eyes with inflammation after exposure to cold
- Pain from the glare of welding or being exposed to ultra-bright glare or snow

Allium cepa
- Bland tears and acrid nasal discharge
- Burning, smarting lacrimation (tearing)
- Sensitivity to light (photophobia)
- Burning eyelids and a desire to rub them
- Swelling around eyes
- Better in open air
- Often experienced during hay fever

Apis
- Swelling of eyelids (oedema), like water bags
- Hot tears with puffy eyes
- Stinging pains
- Better from cool air and bathing
- Light sensitivity (photophobia) worse for covering eyes

Ars alb
- Burning eyes with tears that burn and mark the skin
- Swelling around the eyes
- Red eyelids
- Better for external warmth

Euphrasia
- Copious, acrid, watery or mucous tears that burn the face
- Eyes feel dry and 'as if there is sand in them'
- Bland discharge from the nose
- Blinks a lot
- Can't bear bright light

Merc sol
- Discharge is yellow-green
- Eyes pink and inflamed
- Burning, acrid discharge
- Pain worse at night, and from a warm bed, firelight and sunlight
- Eyelids close spasmodically
- Eye infections with sore throat and colds

Pulsatilla
- Eye infections with or after a cold or flu
- Thick, profuse, bland, yellow-green discharges
- Eyelids inflamed and stick together
- Better for cool applications, cool air
- Styes
- Eyeball can itch and burn

Handy household and herbal hints

Eye inflammations

- Although you can make up a herbal eyebath (*see* below), it is preferable to use commercially manufactured herbal eye drops for their purity. Use commercially available herbal eyedrops containing *Euphrasia* (eyebright) or witch hazel.
- Eyebaths can be made by soaking one tablespoon each of some herbs such as raspberry leaves, marshmallow, eyebright, *Calendula* or fennel in one litre of boiling water. Simmer gently for a few minutes. Allow to cool, strain and use this liquid as an eyebath. Apply fresh liquid to each eye.
- For eyestrain, it is advisable to increase your intake of vitamins A, B and D.
- Eye inflammations are very contagious so keep you child away from school and wash your hands frequently. Everyone in the family should use separate hand towels and face cloths.

EYE INJURIES

This section is included for emergency first-aid treatment while professional help is being sought.

> **Danger facts**
> - **No** injury to the eye should **ever** be neglected. Always gently wash the eye with clean water to clear it of any chemicals or foreign bodies.
> - Never try to remove anything that has punctured the eyeball. Cover the eye and go to an emergency centre immediately.

Aconite
- First remedy for the effects of wounded eyes or foreign bodies in the eyes
- Eyelids are swollen, hard and red, and the eyes look congested
- For the discomfort after extraction of grit, sand or objects from the eye
- Watery, hot discharge from the eyes; the tears running down the face feel hot
- Pupils dilated
- Sensitive to light
- Use immediately after injury for shock and fear

Arnica
- Useful in injuries to the eyeball and to the soft parts of the eye
- Bruising around the eye immediately after the injury (black eye)
- Painful swelling with discoloration
- After an acute blow on the eye causing haemorrhage of the conjunctiva (bleeding in the white of the eye or bloodshot eyes)
- Wants to be left alone, great fear of being touched
- Double vision following injury

Ferrum phos
- Inflammation of soft parts of the eye, localized congestion or haemorrhage
- Better for cold applications
- Blurred vision
- Eyes red and inflamed, with a burning sensation

Ledum
- Contusions (bruises) with a feeling of coldness in the eye
- Bloodshot eyes
- Bruising
- Worse for heat and better for cold applications

Symphytum
- Useful after treating with *Arnica*, when soft parts of the eye have recovered from bruised soreness
- Contusion of the eyeball due to a blow by a fist or blunt object while surrounding tissue remains intact (a black eye)
- Pain in the eyeball
- For discoloration and bruising
- Better from warmth

Handy household and herbal hints

Eye injuries

- It would make sense not to spend time in the sun or to watch television with damaged or painful eyes.
- Place some frozen peas on black eyes, or use ice blocks wrapped in a cloth.
- Bathe eyes in boiled water that has cooled down.
- Make a compress of cotton balls or a clean cloth soaked in a solution of eyebright, chamomile, fennel or *Calendula* infusion or tincture in water and place over the eyes.
- Use tea made from plantain leaf to wet a compress and place it over the eyes – plantain leaf has astringent properties and will be soothing.
- Grated, fresh, raw potato acts as a drying substance and a disinfectant, and can be wrapped in cheesecloth and placed on the eyes.
- Steep some chamomile or rooibos tea bags in boiling water and allow it to cool. Place it on the eyes to reduce swelling.
- You could also use fresh slices of cucumber to reduce swelling – it will be most effective if the cucumber has been in the fridge.

FEVER

Fever is a symptom of the body's response to infections and not an illness. Fever helps to produce interferon, a body chemical that fights infection. The aim of treatment is, therefore, not merely to bring down the sick person's temperature, but to use the symptoms that fever produces as a clue to the individual's reaction.

> **Danger facts**
> If ever in doubt, obtain professional help. Remember that a few characteristic symptoms are sufficient for identification and that you do not need the whole picture. Get help in the following circumstances:
> - Fevers over 39 °C.
> - High fevers in infants.
> - If fever is accompanied by lethargy, confusion, excessive irritability, stiffness of the neck, severe or continued vomiting, laboured, difficult or very shallow breathing.
> - High fever with slow pulse (average adult fever pulse is 90, and in children 120).
> - Pale stools with dark urine.
> - If there is inadequate response to the remedies.

Aconite
- Early beginnings of a fever from cold, dry winds, air conditioning or drinking ice cold drinks regularly during hot weather
- Sudden onset with anxiety and restlessness
- With sweating
- Contracted pupils
- Dry skin, dry cough and dry mouth
- Very thirsty for cold drinks

Ars alb
- Restlessness and anxiety
- Thirst for sips of warm drinks, wants this frequently
- Chilly, wants to be covered and warm
- Worse from midnight to 3 a.m.

- Vomiting and diarrhoea
- Burning pains better for warmth
- Great weakness

Belladonna
- Sudden, high fever; red, flushed face; skin radiates heat and is dry
- First stage of inflammation
- Dilated pupils with staring eyes
- Reddened mucous membranes, for example red mouth, tongue or tonsils
- Bounding pulse
- Overstimulated by fever – children tend to run around wildly; there may even be delirium
- Fever from sun
- Worse at 3 p.m.

Bryonia
- Fever with body pain
- All symptoms are worse for any movement, even breathing or coughing
- Likes hard pressure and warmth on painful parts
- Thirst for large quantities of liquid
- Irritability

Chamomilla
- Irritable, peevish, oversensitive
- One cheek red and hot while the other is cold and pale
- Wants to be carried
- Hot perspiration
- Wants help immediately

Ferrum phos
- For onset of fevers
- For the slow onset of fever
- Symptoms less intense than *Belladonna* (*see* page 51)
- Flushed cheeks
- Nosebleeds

Gelsemium
- For the slow onset of fever
- Dull, dizzy, drowsy and trembling with weakness
- No thirst with fever
- With headache and aching
- Chills up and down the back
- Dull face with droopy eyelids

Ipecac
- Fevers beginning with nausea or vomiting
- No thirst
- Clean tongue

Pulsatilla
- Fever with chilliness
- Worse in a warm room and better for open air
- No thirst
- Changeable symptoms and mood
- Weepy and clingy, wants sympathy and attention
- Children whine and want to be carried
- One cheek red, the other normal or pale

Handy household and herbal hints

Fever

Fever can be a good symptom of the body trying to heal itself. The fever should preferably not be suppressed by antipyretics unless it rises above 39 °C or if the fever presents in a child prone to febrile convulsions.

- Rest and drink plenty of fluid. If the sick person isn't thirsty, let him try sucking crushed ice, or offer him jelly or fruit juice.
- A sponge bath with lukewarm water can be beneficial, but protect the sick person from draughts. Otherwise place cold flannels on his forehead, stomach and feet.
- Take 5–15 drops of *Echinacea* tincture, diluted in water, every two hours.

> **Fever – continued**
> - Prepare elderberry tea by adding three teaspoons of this herb to one litre of boiling water, cover to steep, add honey and sip frequently. This herb promotes perspiration – in fact the tea smells like perspiration!

FOOD POISONING

Food poisoning is a reaction by the body to get rid of spoilt, toxic or infected foods. The body will try to eliminate unwanted substances immediately by vomiting or diarrhoea. However, if this process of elimination continues too long, it may become debilitating and dehydrating. The homoeopathic remedies will aid quick recovery (*see also* Diarrhoea, page 144).

> **Danger fact**
> - Dehydration – if symptoms persist despite treatment and the sick person becomes dehydrated, seek professional help.

Ars alb
- The first remedy to think of for any food poisoning with severe vomiting and diarrhoea. This often occurs simultaneously and after midnight, and is accompanied by intense weakness, exhaustion and collapse. Specifically for poisoning from shellfish and other types of fish, canned food, meat and poultry.
- There can be restlessness, anxiety, worry and even a despair of recovery
- Nausea, retching and vomiting (immediately after eating or drinking), which doesn't alleviate the nausea
- Burning in stomach and abdomen
- Diarrhoea is watery, burning, acrid and foul
- Sick person is very cold and desires to be warm
- She has a thirst for small sips of preferably warm liquid
- Needs company and reassurance

Carbo veg
- Poisoning by food that is slightly off, especially poultry
- Characterized by bloating, indigestion, tremendous passage of wind and gas both upwards and downwards, weakness, collapse, prostration, debility, exhaustion and even fainting
- Chilly but worse for heat, doesn't want to be covered. Wants to be fanned, wants the air conditioner on or wants to lie under an electric fan
- Pale or bluish face, hands and feet
- Sensation of burning on the inside and freezing on the outside
- Food turns to gas that is passed as flatus or eructations (belching), both of which are offensive and afford temporary relief
- Frequent, foul (putrefying) diarrhoea, followed by belching
- Stool is passed with flatus
- Worse for tight clothes around abdomen and waist
- Apathy and indifference

Ipecac
- Intense, violent, constant, incapacitating nausea
- Vomiting that doesn't relieve or aggravates the nausea
- Belching of gas with no taste of food
- Gagging with salivation and sticky mucus
- Not even a drop of water will stay down
- Inclination to sleep after vomiting
- Disgust for food or the smell of food
- No thirst, with clean, uncoated tongue
- Colicky pains with diarrhoea
- Stools are watery, viscous (containing lumps of mucus), putrid and either grass-green or foamy

Nux vom
- Also for the effects of overindulging in food and drink
- The sufferer has a great desire to vomit and a feeling that if she did, she would feel better
- The sick person is irritable, easily angered, short-tempered and finds fault with everything

- Hypersensitive to cold, light, noise, odours and the slightest unpleasantness
- Food sits like a stone in the stomach and remains undigested; the sick person wants to vomit, but cannot, despite trying
- Nausea, vomiting and much retching
- If the retching prevails over the vomiting, *Nux vom* is the best treatment
- Stools – frequent, small evacuations with much urging, with a constant sense of unease in the rectum
- Abdominal cramps

Urtica
- Shellfish poisoning
- Accompanied by urticaria with intense itching, better for warmth

---

Handy household and herbal hints

Food poisoning
- Dehydration must be counteracted by sipping at rehydration fluid, which can be obtained from your local pharmacy. You could also make it yourself by adding one teaspoon of salt, one teaspoon of sugar and one teaspoon of bicarbonate of soda to one litre of water or grapejuice.
- Chamomile tea and ginger powder or slices of the fresh ginger root in boiling water will reduce spasms and gas. *See also* Diarrhoea, page 144.

HAY FEVER

Hay fever is an allergic reaction to pollen causing an inflammation of the mucous membranes of the nose, eyes and throat. It is often accompanied by a lot of sneezing, itching, discharge and irritation of the mucous membranes.

Hay fever should be treated constitutionally and professional help is needed to treat the whole body's overreaction to a minute allergic substance. The following remedies may give you some relief from the acute symptoms, but this must not be confused with a 'cure'. If you are being treated by a professional homoeopath, please check with her before self-prescribing.

> **Danger fact**
> - Nothing significant.

Allium cepa
- The *Allium cepa* hay fever closely resembles an *Allium cepa* cold. There is excessive sneezing and an acrid, burning nasal discharge, as well as a profuse and bland discharge from the eyes
- Eyes are red and burning
- Tickling in the larynx leads to hoarseness and a hacking cough that is worse from inhaling cold air, although the sick person is generally better in the open air

Apis
- Red swelling of nasal passages with bags under the eyes
- Hay fever is often accompanied by urticaria that is better for cold applications

Ars alb
- There is a thin, watery, excoriating nasal discharge with a blocked nose that is not relieved by sneezing
- The hay fever is worse outdoors and better indoors
- Acrid, burning lacrimation (tears)
- Intense sensitivity to light (photophobia)
- Great thirst for frequent sips of warm liquid
- Exhaustion out of proportion to the complaint

Euphrasia
- Fluent, watery discharge from nose and profuse, burning discharge from eyes
- May be accompanied by a violent cough with abundant expectoration and sometimes even by a headache
- Eyes water all the time with sticky mucus in the corners of the eyes
- Better in open air, worse in a warm room and for sunlight

Kali bich
- Pressure and pain in the root of the nose

- Hay fever feels like a cold or sinusitis
- Violent sneezing with a thick, stringy, yellow-green discharge
- Pain behind the eyeballs
- Desires warm drinks

Nat mur
- Violent bouts of sneezing with a watery egg white nasal discharge
- The nose is blocked, loss of smell and taste
- Fever blisters flare up during a cold
- Often better for washing the face with cold water

Nux vom
- This is often a very useful remedy in acute hay fever attacks when it is indicated. However, always check with your homoeopath before taking this remedy as *Nux vom* may counteract your constitutional remedy
- Fluent nasal discharge in the daytime, but the nose feels blocked at night and while out of doors
- Alternate nostrils are blocked
- Acrid discharge, but with blocked feeling that is worse at night
- Rough, scraping tickling in throat, sometimes extending to ears. The sufferer often makes strange noises trying to relieve the itching of the palate and Eustachian tubes
- Feeling of chilliness, great weakness and irritability towards everything
- There may be a desire for warm drinks and a feeling of being very hungry
- Worse after exposure to dry, cold air

Sabadilla
- This is **the** remedy for spasmodic sneezing, which can occur in attacks of over 30 sneezes at a time. It is accompanied by a copiously running and watery nose.
- Eyelids are red and burning, with tearing and watering being worse in the open air
- Nose itches and tickles, and is oversensitive to odours

Silicea
- If not constitutional, *Silicea* hay fevers occur from the exposure to straw and harvesting. Sneezing takes place especially in the morning, with itching in the Eustachian tubes and deep in the ears

> **Handy household and herbal hints**
> **Hay fever**
> - You can reduce the intensity of the symptoms by staying indoors during days with a high pollen count, or keeping the car windows closed. It is also helpful to spray whichever room you are in with a fine atomizing spray (available at plant nurseries) that will settle much of the dust and pollen.
> - Follow a diet low in mucus-producing food, i.e. avoid milk products, refined sugar and wheat during the high-pollen season.
> - Take vitamin C and garlic (or garlic capsules if you don't like garlic) to make the mucous membranes of the nose less sensitive.
> - A tea of elderflower and eyebright herbs will build up the strength of the mucous membranes before the hay fever season.
> - Honey in the comb or propolis from your local area, eaten throughout the winter, reputedly helps to desensitize you to the pollen in the air.

HEADACHES AND MIGRAINES

Headaches and migraines can be caused by many different conditions, varying from flu, stress with neck tension, toothache, menstrual disorders or hormonal imbalances, sensitivity to certain foods like coffee, cheese and chocolate, high or low blood pressure, travel sickness and eyestrain. Less frequently, headaches can also be associated with serious organic diseases.

As we have already mentioned, every headache is different and individual to a person. Therefore you have to be specific with regard to the individual and the reasons for the headache. Remember that there is a big difference between treating acute manifestations of headaches and treating them at a constitutional level. Seek professional homoeopathic help whenever necessary.

> **Danger facts**
> - Headaches that follow a head injury or concussion with nausea, vomiting and drowsiness could indicate internal bleeding. Treat as an emergency.

> **Danger facts – continued**
> - Headaches with fever, light sensitivity (photophobia) and neck stiffness could indicate meningitis. Give the sick person *Belladonna* and *Gelsemium*, and seek immediate help from a hospital.
> - Seek professional help for persistent headaches that are worse in the morning.

Ars alb
- Headaches from midnight to 3 a.m.
- With anxiety and restlessness
- Chilly, but wants cold air on the face
- Headache often accompanies colds and flu

Belladonna
- Headache congestive, throbbing and hammering, with red face
- Intense headache worse from slight noise, jarring, motion, light, lying down and the least bit of exertion
- Better lying on the bed with the head up high on pillows, preferably in the dark with the blinds down or the lights off
- Pain, fullness, especially in forehead
- Headaches often begin in the base of the head, radiate to the right temple or forehead and settle about the right eye
- Rush of blood to the head
- Intense headaches from heatstroke or being out in the sun for too long

Bryonia
- Bursting, splitting headache
- Worse for slightest motion, even of the eyes – even thinking seems to be painful
- Headache over eye or forehead, extending first to the occiput (base of skull) and then to the whole head, better from closing the eyes
- Better from pressure
- Worse from coughing and stooping
- Pressure pains in the occiput, drawing down into the neck
- Headache from constipation

Carbo veg
- Headaches from any overindulgence in rich foods or alcohol
- Head painfully sensitive to pressure, especially of hat; sensation remains after hat is taken off
- Worse from lying flat, overheating
- Desires to be fanned or to have a draught of fresh cool air on himself, despite his chilliness

Gelsemium
- Heavy head and eyelids, feels to the sick person that he can hardly lift either
- Sensation of a band around the head
- Headaches often begin in the occiput or neck and radiate towards the forehead
- Migraine headaches can be preceded by visual disturbances like flickering spots or even temporary blindness
- The headache feels relieved by the passing of urine, which can be profuse
- Muscular soreness of neck and shoulders

Kali bich
- Headache in the root of the nose and frontal sinuses, with aching in the eyeballs
- Headaches accompany colds, sinusitis and hay fever
- *Kali bich* can have a headache with loss of vision at the beginning of a migraine

Mag phos
- Headache begins in occiput and extends over the head
- Headaches from mental exertion
- Better from pressure and external warmth applied to the head
- Likes a scarf for warmth around the neck

Nat mur
- Flickering and visual disturbances before or during a migraine
- Blinding, hammering headache, hammering on the brain
- Numbness and tingling in lips, tongue and nose
- Worse from heat, sun and emotional causes like grief; can also be caused by anxiety in school-going children

Nux vom
- Headache especially after indulgence in alcohol and rich food
- Headache in the morning in bed, just before opening the eyes
- Worse in the morning or from mental exertion, tobacco, alcohol, coffee, open air
- Better from being in a warm room, sitting quietly or lying down

Pulsatilla
- Headache from daytime movies or from being in a stuffy room
- Headache is better for walking around slowly in cool air
- With weepy mood and other *Pulsatilla* symptoms

Handy household and herbal hints

Headaches and migraines

At a less specific level, here are some herbal remedies that can offer relief.

For tension or nervous headaches:
- Rub lavender water or eau de Cologne on the forehead
- Rosemary tea with a pinch of marjoram can be helpful for the relief of tension and the circulation of blood to the head, and can help the liver get rid of toxins. Infuse one large tablespoon of the herbs in one litre of boiling water. Allow to cool in a covered container. Drink one cupful hourly.
- Meadowsweet and willow herb contain natural aspirin, although in very small quantities. However, they are still effective in reducing the pain of a headache. Take two teaspoons of the dried herb in a large mug of boiling water. Sweeten as required.
- Valerian root relaxes and relieves neuralgic pains with tension. Take 20 drops in some water every two hours.
- Make some ordinary Indian tea with one or two cloves in the teapot. Drink as you would ordinary tea.

For migraines or headaches associated with liver problems:
- Infuse a pinch each of some vervain, cinnamon, basil and thyme in a cup of boiling water. Allow to cool and drink.

> **For migraines or headaches associated with liver problems – continued**
> - Feverfew can relieve migraines and lengthen the time between attacks. Take as herbal tincture drops (15 drops in water 3 times a day) or eat three leaves in a sandwich daily.
> - Combine some of the following herbs (one teaspoonful each) and use to make a tea – vervain, betony, ground ivy, rosemary, skullcap, lavender, marjoram or sage.

HEATSTROKE

Heatstroke is a reaction to excessive exposure to heat or the sun, together with dehydration.

> **Danger facts**
> - Confusion, disorientation, rapid pulse, shallow breathing.
> - Dehydration and shock.
> - Heatstroke can lead to unconsciousness, so if in doubt, seek professional help immediately.

Aconite

- Onset is sudden and intense
- Some degree of anxiety, fear or shock
- Panic to the point of overwhelming terror of death
- Often given as a first remedy and then followed by others
- Restlessness
- Headaches caused by exposure to sun
- Great thirst, usually for cold drinks
- Skin is red, hot, swollen, dry, burning and shining
- The sick person's skin may feel cold, or he may feel prickles as from needles here and there
- May begin with bouts of shivering
- Strong pulse

Belladonna
- Onset is sudden and intense
- Burning heat, dilated pupils (shiny, staring, glazed eyes)
- Skin is red, and either dry or damp with hot perspiration
- Delirium, hallucinations or convulsions
- Temperature high and fluctuates
- Strong pulse
- Throbbing pains, especially in head and severe headache
- Worse for light, noise, jolts
- Better from rest
- Exhaustion and/or restlessness
- Usually no thirst, but may want lemonade or lemon

Carbo veg
- Person is in a state of extreme weakness or collapse
- Cold and pale with cold breath, cold tongue and cold sweat
- Needs air – wants to be fanned (to lie under an electric fan or air conditioner)
- Worse from heat despite being cold
- Feels hot inside but cold outside
- Weak digestion with bloating, flatulence (winds) and belching

Gelsemium
- Slower onset
- Weariness, weakness, sleepiness, fatigue, 'can't be bothered'
- A dull, listless feeling with heavy, drooping eyelids
- Stiffness and muscular aches
- Trembling (internal and/or external)
- Often has diarrhoea with the heatstroke
- Face is crimson
- No thirst
- Much urination
- May show signs of shock
- Weak pulse

Nat mur
- Easy heatstroke from the sun
- With blinding, throbbing headache, as if a thousand little hammers were knocking on the brain
- Paleness, nausea and vomiting with headache
- Headaches characteristically occur at 10 a.m.
- Sneezing and runny nose from the sun
- Unquenchable thirst for cold drinks

Rhus tox
- Heatstroke after getting wet while perspiring in the heat
- Heatstroke after exertion in the heat
- Often with muscular strain or stiffness
- Intense thirst for cold water or milk (will tend to drink in sips)
- Prostration with restlessness or restless legs
- Red triangle at tip of tongue
- Skin is dry, burning and itching

Handy household and herbal hints

Heatstroke
- Sponge down the affected person with cool water and treat as for fevers.
- Make sure that she drinks sufficient liquid to prevent dehydration and further problems. Grape juice is rich in potassium and will alleviate the feelings of weakness.
- Lemon and honey drinks can reduce the fever, as can infusions of elderberry flowers and lime flowers.

INJURIES

This is a summary of general injuries – for more specific injuries, *see* Bites and stings (page 116), Burns (page 124) and Eye injuries (page 160).

> **Danger signs that might need medical intervention:**
> - Animal or human bites that puncture deeper than the skin and become septic
> - Any deep puncture wound, even if the surface is small,
> - Any wound showing signs of infection, pus and redness, and with a red line going up the limb from the wound or swelling
> - A ragged wound usually scars, so if it is on an area that you don't wish to scar, for instance the face, have it stitched by a plastic surgeon,
> - A dirty wound that you cannot clean completely,
> - Wounds on joints where scarring would limit movement, for example bending the elbow,
> - Cuts on the hand – check that the fingers can move and have feeling in them as the nerves and tendons are often affected and surgery may be indicated,
> - Excessive bleeding,
> - No tetanus injection for the last 12 months and the wound has been in contact with soil or horses,

Aconite

- Any injury accompanied by fear, anxiety and restlessness
- Intense pain
- Sudden onset
- The '*Arnica*' of the eye – use if the eyes are red, dry and hot, also useful after extraction of cinders or foreign bodies from the eye
- From snow reflection, the glare of a welder's torch and dry, cold winds
- Haemorrhage of bright red blood, e.g. nosebleeds

Apis

- Bee stings
- Swelling after bites, sore and stinging, rosy colour
- Better for cold applications

Arnica

- After accidents, strains, overuse of any organ
- Falls, blows, bruising and bleeding

- After strokes, spinal concussion
- Acts on soft tissue
- Helpful postoperatively and after childbirth
- Bedsores
- Concussion
- Do not apply to broken skin
- Do not use *Arnica* if the injured person is on prescribed blood thinners

Bellis perennis
- Injuries to deeper tissue after surgery or childbirth
- Injuries to nerves, with intense soreness
- Worse for cold bathing
- Sprains and bruises
- Lameness as if sprained, e.g. after gardening
- Blows to breast or from the impact of a seatbelt slamming into male or female breast tissue in car accidents
- Bloated rumbling in bowels postoperatively

Calendula
- Antiseptic – disinfects open wounds and grazes
- Acts as a styptic, that is it stops bleeding when you dab the tincture onto dry cotton wool and apply it with pressure to the bleeding area. If you dilute the tincture, you can put it on gauze and apply to burns. Keep it moist with the diluted tincture
- Use as a gargle and mouthwash. Stops bleeding after tooth extraction
- Use in potency (for example 6ch or 30ch) for sepsis

Cantharis
- Severe burns or sunburn with blistering

Hypericum
- Injuries to nerves, especially where many nerves are present, for example fingers, toes, nail bed or mouth
- Crushed fingertips, for example from car doors
- Puncture wounds and animal bites
- Postoperatively it reduces pain

- Falls injuring the coccyx (tail bone)
- Effects of shock
- Sensitive wounds
- Laceration wounds with weakness from loss of blood
- Excessive painfulness

Ledum
- Puncture wounds, stings, bites, splinters, bruises and stepping on sharp foreign bodies
- Bruised eye wounds
- The wounded part often feels cold
- Chilly, but dislikes the heat of the bed, better from cold air and cold applications

Rhus tox
- Ailments from strains and lifting heavy objects, with tearing pains
- Antidote to poison ivy poisoning or any plant-induced allergic rash (6ch or 30ch potencies work well), which is better for warm to hot bathing
- Affects fibrous tissue in tendons, ligaments and around joints
- Postoperatively it can be very useful if there is great restlessness

Ruta
- Strains, especially to flexor tendons, e.g. repetitive strain injuries of musicians and people who work on computers
- Overstrain of eye muscles
- Lameness after sprains
- Injured, bruised bones, and fractures

Silicea
- Helps expel foreign bodies and splinters when used in a low potency (6ch)

Symphytum
- Injuries to tendons and periosteum (membranous lining around bones)
- Wounds penetrating to periosteum and bone, and fractures that do not knit and heal
- Traumatic eye injuries or pain in the eye after a blow

Urtica

- Burns or scalds – apply as a dressing, keeping it covered and moist with *Urtica*, and use the potency internally
- Bleeding wounds and nosebleeds

Injury table

	Aconite	Apis	Arnica	Calendula	Cantharis	Hypericum	Ledum	Rhus tox	Ruta	Symphytum	Urtica
Puncture wounds	-	-	-	-	-	+	+	-	-	-	-
Injuries to spine	-	-	+	-	-	+	-	-	-	-	-
Eye injuries	+	-	-	-	-	-	+	-	+	+	-
Fractures	-	-	+	+	-	+	-	-	+	+	-
Burns	-	-	-	+	+	-	-	-	-	-	+
Bedsores	-	-	+	+	-	-	-	-	-	-	-
Bites	-	+	+	-	+	+	+	+	-	-	+
Concussion	+	-	+	-	-	+	-	-	-	-	-
Open wounds, scrapes	-	-	-	+	-	+	-	-	-	-	-

Handy household and herbal hints

Injuries

A bruise is an internal haemorrhage or bleed caused by an impact or bang against a harder object. The internal bleeding can cause pain, swelling and discoloration of the skin.

- Apply cabbage leaves, dipped in hot water and bruised, to the bruised area as they relieve congestion.

> **Injuries – continued**
> - Make a compress of various individual or combined herbs – try marigold, witch hazel, melilot (sweet clover), nettle or comfrey. Pour boiling water over two teaspoonfuls of the herb(s). Leave for 10 minutes and, when cool, moisten a cool compress and apply over the bruised area. Moisten again frequently.
> - Mix a paste of pounded marjoram leaves with honey and apply it to the bruise to reduce the discoloration.

MEASLES
see Children's infectious diseases, page 127

MENOPAUSE
see Women's ailments, page 194

MIGRAINES
see Headaches and migraines, page 170

MOUTH ULCERS AND DENTAL PROBLEMS
Mouth ulcers are painful denuded areas in the tongue, gums, palate or inner lips. These are common affections that can occur from babyhood onwards.

> **Danger fact**
> - Nothing significant.

Ars alb
- Unhealthy gums that bleed easily and are painful to touch
- Ulceration of mouth with dryness and burning
- There may be an increased thirst for sips of warm water
- The tongue is dry, clean and red, and the ulcers may have a blue hue
- Improved by warmth
- Sometimes water tastes bitter

Hepar sulph
- Ulcers of the soft palate (roof of mouth at the back) and ulcers on insides of the lips, cheeks and tongue
- The gums and mouth are painful from the slightest touch and bleed easily, and there may be an increase in the amount of saliva produced
- The ulcer pain is better from warmth and heat

Kali bich
- The ulcers look punched out

Merc sol
- All types of ulcers in mouth and on the tongue
- There is inflammation and superficial ulceration of the mucous membranes of the mouth; these mucous membranes are spongy, slimy-looking and bluish-red
- The gums become inflamed, swollen and bleed easily
- The tongue is large, flabby, shows the imprint of the teeth and is often coated
- There may be a metallic taste in the mouth
- Offensive breath and excessive saliva

Nat mur
- Mouth ulcers with vesicles and burning of the tongue, with bubbles on the tongue
- The gums are spongy and bleed easily
- The tongue may be 'mapped' with red patches and resemble an atlas
- There is a sense of dryness in the mouth

Handy household and herbal hints

Mouth ulcers and dental problems

Recurrent mouth ulcers and inflammations of the gums can be signs of gum disease or incorrect dental hygiene. Contact your dentist or dental hygienist for a check-up.
- To protect your teeth and gums, avoid sugars, refined starches and carbonated drinks. Make sure that you eat enough fresh fruit and vegetables daily, and get sufficient exercise and sleep.

- For dental problems, consider supplementing your diet with extra vitamin C and calcium.
- For mouth ulcers use a *Calendula* tincture (15 drops in a little warm water) or make a warm *Calendula* infusion (made as a tea) and use as a gargle, swishing it around the mouth every hour.
- Use a powder made from goldenseal and place directly onto the mouth ulcer with a cotton bud.
- Three drops of *Myrrh* tincture in a glass of warm water, gargled every one or two hours, heals most mouth ulcers very rapidly.
- Marshmallow root or comfrey root releases a mucilaginous gel when chewed or simmered in water. This gel is soothing, lubricating, healing and eases pain. Make a strong tea of the leaves or root and use it as a mouthwash for mouth ulcers and gumboils.
- Make a mouthwash by soaking one handful of wintergreen leaves in two cups of apple cider vinegar for 24 hours. Dilute with one cup of water and strain out the wintergreen. Store in the fridge and use as necessary.
- Chew a clove to relieve toothache while waiting to see your dentist.

MUMPS
see Children's infectious diseases, page 127

PREGNANCY
see Women's ailments, page 197

SHOCK
It is important to treat shock as it can retard healing. The shock can linger and become debilitating and lead to post traumatic stress syndrome.

Danger fact
- Always monitor the reactions of a shocked person. If there is a lot of hysteria, you may need to obtain professional assistance.

Aconite
- After any acute shock or fright
- The person becomes extremely anxious. He is restless, fears death and feels that he is in great and imminent danger
- He becomes frantic, screams and groans, and has a look of extreme terror on his face. The face is flushed and the pulse full, hard and rapid, caused by a sudden and intense fear
- There is a sudden and great loss of strength
- Intense thirst for large quantities of cold water
- Improves with the onset of sweating
- Faints when rising after lying down

Arnica
- After traumatic injuries, for example a car accident
- The sick person says there is nothing the matter with him – 'I am all right'. He sends the doctor home and refuses X-rays and treatment
- Wants to be left alone, is unwilling even to be spoken to
- Fears touch
- He must lie down, yet the bed feels too hard – keeps moving from place to place in search of a softer spot
- Limbs and body ache as if beaten
- Sore, lame, bruised feeling
- For the trauma of grief and shock

Carbo veg
- Physical collapse from any cause – administer while seeking professional help
- Desires moving air and to be fanned
- Paleness, blueness and weak pulse

Gelsemium
- The shocked person wants to be held because he is shaking and trembling badly
- Prefers to be quiet, but hates to be alone
- Feels physically weak and drained, as if his strength is being drained by the heaviness in all his limbs
- Better from passing large amounts of urine

- Better from sweating and alcoholic stimulants
- No thirst
- Dizzy and drowsy

Ignatia
- Appropriate following emotional shocks such as sad events, grief, mourning, accidents, disappointments and for nervous conditions of emotional origin
- Hypersensitive, with sighing, fainting, sobbing
- The individual desires to be alone, to sit and brood in silence and grief, but is actually better from distraction
- Contradictory and paradoxical symptoms present, for example crying fits may turn into laughing fits or the giggles
- The shocked person is highly emotional, nervous and tearful and has changeable mood swings
- General hypersensitivity to pain and to smells, especially tobacco

---

Handy household and herbal hints

Shock

- Administer *Rescue Remedy* frequently and allow the shocked person to cry or repeatedly tell her story if she wishes to do so. This often relieves some of the feelings she may have bottled up.
- Keep the shocked person warm – chamomile tea sweetened with honey will be soothing.
- Do not leave the shocked person alone. Nurture her with tender care.
- A few drops of essential oils of lavender, bergamot, lemon balm or chamomile in a warm bath, or inhaled or rubbed into the feet are calming and relaxing.
- Herb teas like skullcap, *verbena*, *passiflora* and *Avena sativa* help to nourish the nervous system and reduce strain.
- Kava kava tablets taken four times a day for a week or more after the event causing the shock can help to ease associated anxiety.

SINUSITIS AND CATARRH

Sinusitis is caused by a swelling of the mucous membranes of the upper respiratory tract and sinus cavities in the head. This occurs when the mucous membranes lining the canals and inner cavities of the nose, throat, head and ears become inflamed, sore and red. The membranes then produce a discharge or catarrh that is first watery and later becomes thicker and stickier. The normal function of these membranes is to remove the dust and germs from the air we inhale and to warm it before it enters the delicate passages of the lungs.

Viruses that bring about head colds can cause the mucous membranes to continue discharging mucus and catarrh. This can last for a long time and become chronic or turn into a secondary infection, and result in sinusitis. Headaches can occur from blocked or infected sinus cavities. The mucus that pours down the back of the throat is called a postnasal drip or discharge.

Sinusitis presents with pressure in the nose; under and above the eyes, sometimes with pain or a feeling of stuffiness in the nose and face. There can be a dull, continuous headache. It can be caused by a cold or allergies to certain foods, for instance dairy products or excess sugar, white flour and colourants. Air pollution, dust or pollen can also set off a sinus congestion, inflammation and infection.

Danger facts
- Very severe pain, fever.
- Very offensive nasal discharge.
- Foreign objects up nasal passages.

Hepar sulph
- The pain is worse for the slightest touch and for anything cold
- The sick person wants a scarf or hat on the head
- Pain is concentrated at the root of the nose
- The head and face feel bruised and sore even when touched lightly
- Pain is worse for movement of the eyes
- Sneezes in cold wind, or nose gets blocked
- Postnasal drip
- Helps promote discharge

Kali bich
- Pressure, fullness and pain at the root of the nose
- Headache improved by runny or discharging nose
- Pain in small spots, for example in bone under arch of eyebrow
- Loss of smell
- Discharge thick, stringy, sticky, greenish-yellow, sometimes jelly-like
- It can be blown out of the nose or forms a postnasal drip, which can sometimes be hawked up
- Crusts in the nose can be yellow, brown and bloody; feel like they need to be detached
- Nose blocked, with violent sneezing

Merc sol
- Pain extends from sinuses to teeth or is felt only in the teeth
- Discharge bloody, yellow-green
- Sore, raw, ulcerated nostrils
- Nose bleeds at night
- Sneezes in sunshine
- Thirsty, chilly, sweaty and weak
- Has a 'cloudy' head

Nat mur
- Violent, watery cold with much sneezing, followed by a blocked nose
- Discharge like raw egg white
- Loss of smell and taste
- Inflammation in frontal sinuses
- Dry sinusitis
- Intense pain from root of nose to forehead

Pulsatilla
- One nostril blocked with thick, bland, copious white or yellow mucus
- The mucus has a bad smell to the sick person
- Nasal bones sore
- Changeable symptoms
- Better in open air

Silicea
- All sinuses are involved
- Headache in forehead
- Tip of nose itches, rubs nose vigorously
- Sneezes in the morning
- Hard crusts of mucus in the nose that bleed when loosened
- Swelling between and above the eyebrows
- Discharges infected, yellow-green, offensive, bloody and can be bland
- Dizziness, with sinusitis that is worse looking upwards
- Desires warmth to the head
- Pain better from pressure on the forehead
- Pain worse from noise, cold and stooping
- Itching in Eustachian tubes
- Pain in facial bones

> **Handy household and herbal hints**
> **Sinusitis and catarrh**
> - Take garlic daily. For an adult, swallow four capsules two to three times a day during an acute attack, or one clove of garlic cut up in pieces or crushed and taken with a little juice or in a teaspoon of honey. During an acute attack, do this up to three times a day. Any garlic smell on the body will disappear after 10 days as the body's chemistry adapts to the garlic. Known as 'Russian penicillin', garlic has the added advantage of being antiseptic. It also reduces cholesterol levels while it is taken.
> - Lemon juice and honey, swallowed as often as desired, reduces mucous secretions.
> - Combine some of the following herbs to make a useful tea: elderflower, sage, goldenrod, yarrow, eyebright, peppermint and thyme. Add two teaspoons of each of the dried herbs chosen to approximately one litre of boiling water. Strain and drink a cup three to four times a day until the catarrh clears.
> - Goldenrod, garlic, eyebright and elderflower are all anticatarrhal and act as an astringent to the mucous membranes.

> **Dietary advice**
> - Avoid white sugar, white flour, milk and cheese products, sweets and chocolates.
> - Eat fresh fruit and vegetables, and fresh salads.
> - Alcohol, especially beer and wine, and some soft drinks containing sulphur dioxide as a preservative, can cause further congestion and a sensation of a blocked nose and ears.
> - Smoking and smoky atmospheres can aggravate and irritate the nasal mucous membranes, causing them to produce excess and chronic catarrh.
>
> **Inhalations**
> - Inhale vapour of 10 drops eucalyptus oil in 1 litre of boiling water.
> - Inhale the steam and vapour of one teaspoon each of dried thyme, chamomile and dried peppermint in one litre of boiling water.

SORE THROATS

Sore throats can be caused by allergies, infections or the effects of a postnasal discharge. They often accompany colds and flu.

> **Danger facts**
> - Seek professional help in the following circumstances:
> - If there is such severe throat pain that it prevents swallowing, eating and drinking.
> - If the sick person has difficulty breathing.
> - If the sore throat is accompanied by a high fever and a red, rough rash.
> - If there is an abscess on the tonsils.
> - If the sick person has previously had rheumatic fever.

Apis

- Oedematous swelling of uvula; swollen uvula looks like a sac of water
- The throat is a bright pinky-red
- Pains are burning, darting, stinging and better for cold
- No thirst

- Worse for all forms of heat, touch and pressure
- Great sensitivity to touch on the neck
- Fiery red margin round the upper throat
- Gums and lips swollen
- Better for uncovering, cool air and cold bathing

Belladonna
- Early stages of inflammations
- Throat, tongue and tonsils bright red, sometimes with the beginning of small white patches
- Burning pain
- Strawberry tongue, that is a white-coated tongue with red papillae of the tongue showing through
- Constant desire to drink cold water, but swallowing is painful so sick person sips the water
- Pain and inflammation more likely to be on the right side of the thoat
- Sudden onset of symptoms, becoming severe quickly
- Red, flushed face
- Hot, dry, red skin and mucous membranes
- High fevers even to the point of delirium, and with intense heat
- Shiny eyes with dilated pupils, light sensitivity (photophobia)
- Hot head with cold limbs
- Hypersensitive to jarring, touch, pressure and light
- Worse at 3 p.m. or 3 a.m.

Hepar sulph
- Pain pricking, sharp or sticking like a splinter or fish bone
- Pain extends to the ear
- Warm drinks bring some relief to throat pain
- Chilly
- Sweat profuse and offensive
- Pus formation on tonsils
- Catarrh, sometimes with a barking cough
- Hypersensitive, irritable, quarrelsome, impatient
- Overreacts to draughts and cold in general

Kali bich

- Relaxed, swollen uvula (little tongue) hanging down
- White or yellow stringy mucus hanging down the back of the throat like two strings
- Postnasal drip
- Discharges are tough, stringy, lumpy and yellow-green
- Sore throat better for warmth
- Mouth ulcers

Merc sol

- Sore throat extends to the ears on swallowing and infections tend to go to the chest
- Increased saliva and dribbling during sleep, often with intense thirst for cold water, fizzy drinks or milk
- Slimy-looking throat without pus, from viral infection
- Can have pus or suppuration
- Mouth feels dry though the tongue looks moist
- Swollen cervical lymph glands
- Sore throat, sometimes relieved by cold drinks and ice cream, sometimes by warm liquids
- Flabby, slimy tongue indented with tooth marks along the edge
- Offensive breath
- Hypersensitive to both heat and cold – hot one minute and cold the next
- Perspiration profuse and offensive, does not bring any relief
- Restlessness with weakness, an internal trembling feeling
- Night aggravations

Nux vom

- Rawness, roughness or tightness of throat
- Tickling in the throat after waking in the morning
- Itching in Eustachian tubes, stitching pain in ears
- Catarrhal hoarseness with scraping in throat
- Irritability, impatience
- Sensitive to touch, pain, smell, noise, music, drugs … life in general!
- Chilly
- Hungry

Silicea
- Pus formation on tonsils and ears
- Often used after treatment with *Hepar sulph* to complete healing in stubborn tonsillitis
- Persistently swollen lymph glands
- Lingering infection accompanied by weakness, low vitality and tendency to relapse
- Perspiration on hands, feet or head smells unpleasant and is profuse
- Chilly, wants to be covered with a scarf and hat
- Worse for any draught or chill, especially on the head
- Feels very sensitive, weepy and needy
- Can be obstinate

> **Handy household and herbal hints**
> **Sore throats**
> - Use *Phytolacca* tincture, 5–10 drops in half a glass of water, for gargling every two hours. Swallow after gargling.
> - Steep three teaspoons of dried sage in one litre of boiling water. Cover and allow to cool. Gargle and swallow.
> - Mix hot lemon and honey with a little grated ginger root and drink often.
> - Consider *Echinacea* or *Baptisia* tincture – use 5–15 drops in warm water every two hours, gargle and swallow.
> - Mix 10–20 drops of *Calendula* tincture with warm water and gargle every two hours – swallow the mixture. Also use as a preventative if exposed to others' coughs and colds.
> - Take vitamin C or use zinc lozenges as per the manufacturer's instructions.

STINGS
see Bites and stings, page 116

TEETHING
see Children's ailments, page 126

URTICARIA

This section is included for the treatment of acute allergic reactions on the skin. Urticaria, other skin eruptions and dermatitis are in fact constitutional problems and will therefore need professional assistance. Urticaria is commonly known as 'hives'.

> **Danger fact**
> - If large parts of the body or the throat become swollen, seek immediate professional help.

Apis
- Urticaria from bee stings or stings from other insects, accompanied by swelling (oedema), severe itching and stinging, which can be worse at night
- Bites covered with large, elevated white weals
- Skin colour rosy
- Better for cold applications

Nat mur
- White hives on arms and hands
- Itching, pricking and burning of skin
- Itching after exertion or becoming hot

Rhus tox
- Urticaria during heat worse from cold air, from getting wet and from contact with certain plants like poison ivy, stinging nettle, and so on
- The itch feels much better for hot, even scalding hot water

Urtica
- Itching blotches
- Urticaria burning, prickling and hot with violent itching
- From ill effects of shellfish
- The urticaria is sometimes accompanied by pale, transparent blisters
- Warmth can often bring some relief

> **Handy household and herbal hints**
> **Urticaria**
> - Urtica tincture on weals
> - Vitamin C (250 mg every four hours) stabilizes the allergic reaction.
> - An infusion of equal parts of yarrow, *Echinacea*, chamomile, peppermint and red clover will strengthen the immune system, reduce swelling and encourage lymph drainage. The mixture can be applied to the skin too.
> - Rooibos tea in bath water can alleviate itching, as can the milky substance that comes out of oats when you pour boiling water over it. It is best to place a handful of oats into an old sock, pour boiling water over it and add this milky substance to the bath water. The surface of the sock will become slimy and mucilaginous and this is also soothing when rubbed gently onto the skin.

WOMEN'S AILMENTS

Most of the remedies described in this section are found in the remedy section (*see* pages 41–107). We have included a few other remedies that are specific to women's ailments as well.

MENOPAUSE

Menopause can be treated very successfully with homoeopathy. For the best results, or in difficult cases, we cannot overemphasize how beneficial it could be to obtain the aid of a professional homoeopath as much of the prescribing is constitutional. For mild cases that may need little intervention, the discussion below will be useful. The basic premise is that menopause is a natural transition of the body and not a disease in process.

Menopause usually occurs between the ages of 45 and 55. During this transitional phase, menstruation becomes irregular, diminished or increase in flow, and then ceases altogether – hence the word *meno-pause*. Periods have to be absent for one year before you can say that you are postmenopausal.

Symptoms can arise during the premenopausal and in the peri- or postmenopausal stage. The most commonly encountered symptoms are hot flushes, perspiration, insomnia, weight gain, mood swings and vaginal dryness. Except in very few cases, most women can handle this natural hormonal transition with the aid of phyto-oestrogenic herbs (phyto-oestrogens) and foodstuffs, and homoeopathic remedies. HRT (hormone replacement therapy) has received a lot of publicity because of its dangers and negative side effects. Every woman should make a fully informed decision before utilizing HRT.

Remedies

For mood changes and insomnia: *Aconite*, *Chamomilla*, *Ignatia*, *Nux vom* and *Pulsatilla*
For hot flushes: *Belladonna*, *Pulsatilla*, *Sepia* and *Sanguinaria*

Plants and foods

There are many plants and foods that contain substances called phyto-oestrogens – the best-known ones are listed below.

- *Angelica sinensis*, or Dong Quai, is a herb that is well documented for use in menopause. It has been utilized as a tonic and spice in Chinese medicine for thousands of years. It seems to have a marked effect on vitamin E utilization and is very useful for irregular menstruation, dysmenorrhoea (painful periods) and during the menopausal period.
- *Cimicifuga racemosa*, the black cohosh, has long been considered a natural alternative to oestrogen replacement in menopausal disorders. Clinical studies have shown that it relieves not only hot flushes, but also depression and vaginal atrophy, heart palpitations, headaches, night sweats, anxiety, sleep disturbances and decreased libido associated with menopause.
- *Dioscorea* (wild yam) specially formulated in a cream can be absorbed through the skin into the fat cells. It is useful in premenstrual tension with its symptoms of emotional withdrawal, sexual disinterest, swollen and lumpy breasts and frequent urination. At menopause, *Dioscorea* has been documented to assist where there are symptoms with hot flushes, vaginal dryness, treatment of mild joint and muscle aches and rheumatism. Eczema and dermatitis with a hormonal component respond favourably.
- *Verbena officinalis*, or vervain, is mildly oestrogenic in action. It also has an effect on the liver, moderately increasing the flow of bile. It is mood elevating,

calming fussiness, a critical nature and irritability. It banishes 'the blues'. It has a calming, restorative effect on the nervous system, which may well be indicated during the menopausal, transitional period of time.
- *Vitex agnus castus*, the chaste berry, promotes menstruation and induces lactation in new mothers. This herb is considered specific for any form of premenstrual tension and is also indicated for hot flushes, diminished libido during menopause and for uterine fibroids, ovarian cysts and mild endometriosis. The recommended dosage is 40 drops of alcohol extract daily in the morning. Variations on this appear to be effective as well, but the herb must be taken for several weeks before an effect can be seen. It is safe to continue for many months.
- *Trifolium pratense*, or red clover, contains phyto-oestrogenic isoflavones similar to those of soya products, which have shown positive effects in increasing bone density. No negative side effects have been found, and numerous trials are currently being conducted on products made from red clover and from soya derivatives.

Other helpful factors

- To ensure a smooth menopausal transition, follow a healthy diet including large amounts of fresh fruits and vegetables, soya products, nuts and natural grains and cereals. Avoid soda drinks containing phosphoric acid, artificial colourings and preservatives that leach calcium from the bones. You should also avoid white sugar, refined products, alcohol (take it in moderation if you do), fats and coffee. Plants like soya, fennel, parsley and celery are rich in phyto-oestrogens, which help the whole system in this hormonal transition.
- Supplement your diet with additional vitamin E (400iu), vitamin C (500 mg twice a day), a comprehensive calcium/magnesium supplement with boron to protect and maintain bone health, and a good multivitamin and mineral supplement. Eat 12 almonds a day for extra calcium and take *Calc phos* and *Calc fluor* tissue salts to aid the absorption and retention of essential minerals. Vitamin B complex, evening primrose oil and flaxseed oil are also recommended.
- Vitamin E capsules, inserted vaginally, have been shown to alleviate vaginal dryness.

- Regular weight-bearing exercise is necessary for bone and cardiovascular health.
- Walking, yoga and Tai Chi will help to maintain postural balance.

MENSTRUATION

The onset of menstruation occurs in puberty and continues until the menopause. Menstruation ceases during pregnancy. Menstrual disorders at all ages and stages can be treated very effectively with homoeopathy, but the treatment should be undertaken by a professional homoeopath.

For first-aid situations, refer to Cramps and Colic (*see* page 142) for painful menstruation. Please refer to the appropriate sections in the book for other problems like headaches (*see* page 170) and mood changes (*see* Emotional states, page 152).

PREGNANCY

One of the major benefits of homoeopathy during pregnancy is that it is **completely safe**. It can be used with the absolute assurance that there will be no iatrogenic effects (drug-induced illnesses and side effects) on the developing foetus.

> **Danger signs during pregnancy**
> **Seek professional help *at once* if any of the following occurs:**
> - Vaginal bleeding, with or without urinary symptoms such as frequent, painful urination, fever and generalized malaise, as it could be an indication of a pending miscarriage, an ectopic pregnancy or placenta praevia.
> - Continuous and severe abdominal pain that does not respond to your chosen remedy within a few hours – this could indicate an ectopic pregnancy.
> - Persistent and quite severe backache around or just above the waist, with or without urinary symptoms, could indicate a kidney infection.
> - Regular and increasingly severe contractions before the due date could herald a premature delivery.
> - The baby stops moving completely or slows down its movement dramatically.
> - Headaches with visual blurring or chest pain and/or swelling of both hands and face could indicate toxaemia.
> - Leaking of waters before being in labour or before due date.
> - Severe anxiety or depression.

In the remedy section, we have given you a general overview of the remedies and their essential actions. However, remedy pictures are much larger than those given in this book. Therefore we have supplied more details below at the specific level of pregnancy to broaden your knowledge of their actions as applied to women.

Arnica

- The first remedy to consider after childbirth or a Caesarian section
- Sore, bruised pain from a very active baby
- Lessens the pains after birth
- A sensation of feeling bruised from within

Belladonna

- '*Belladonna* is especially suited to women in labour having a first baby in their late 30s or 40s. They rant, rage and quarrel with everyone, becoming uncontrollably angry with the pains. Under stress, anger surfaces more easily than fear.' M. Castro
- During breastfeeding the breasts can be swollen, red or red-streaked, engorged, hot and hard
- There is an abundant milk supply, with throbbing, congested breasts as the milk comes in
- Breast abscesses tend to form – seek professional help

Bellis perennis

- In pregnancy abdominal pains can be sudden, with a sore feeling in the uterus caused by the growing baby stretching the uterine ligaments
- Deeper acting than *Arnica* and useful after childbirth in those cases where *Arnica* has not alleviated the bruised soreness
- Useful for lumps remaining even after very old injuries
- Sudden groin pains and weak legs in pregnancy, especially after the baby's head has engaged

Bryonia

- At the end of pregnancy, when muscles are stretched and vulnerable to strain, there can be pain in the lower back that is worse from motion

Caulophyllum
- Labour is late and slow, the cervix doesn't soften and the labour pains last for too short a time and are too weak to enable dilation of the cervix; labour pains tend to slow down
- Labour pains fly around the body and can be felt in the groin, legs and bladder
- Contractions are short and very painful
- Exhaustion and trembling with chilliness, even when covered up, accompany the labour
- Using low potency *Caulophyllum*, that is in a 6ch potency a month before labour, helps to soften the cervix

Chamomilla
- The keynote of the woman needing *Chamomilla* is oversensitivity, both mentally and physically. The woman becomes hypersensitive to her labour pains and quarrelsome, demanding immediate intervention and pain relief
- Labour pains are felt in the back and the woman feels exhausted
- The slow dilation of the cervix makes her angry, impatient and unable to cope with the pain

Cimicifuga
- The *Cimicifuga* woman feels very depressed and is fearful for her health and safety, as well as that of the baby. She fears the birth and feels that she is going crazy
- The labour pains are unbearable and are felt in the groin, the back, hips or they move from one side of the abdomen to the other
- The cervix may not soften, and the labour pains may stop or become weak
- Symptoms are all worse for cold
- In the last months of pregnancy, the woman needing *cimicifuga* can have severe Braxton Hicks contractions (false contractions)

Gelsemium
- Anticipatory anxiety about the birth
- Her body feels heavy and she trembles with exhaustion
- The labour pains are often false, weak and ineffectual
- Backache in labour

- The woman becomes apathetic, despairing and fearful
- This remedy is especially indicated for the transition phase of labour when the woman feels she can no longer go on

Nat mur
- Appetite diminished during pregnancy
- Depressed in pregnancy but unable to cry because of suppressed emotions and grief, or tends to cry alone. She may become introverted and tearful
- A useful remedy to give just before labour because it can help some women achieve transition in labour and emotionally from one phase of their lives to the new one that they are entering

Nux vom
- Premature labours arise severely in the back, but they can also stop suddenly if the cervix doesn't dilate
- The woman can have an urging to pass a stool and a desire to vomit or retch during labour pains, along with the typical *Nux vom* irritable, emotional state

Phytolacca
- Breasts are inflamed, lumpy, painful and swollen
- This remedy is specific for sore, cracked nipples where the pain radiates from the nipple to other parts of the body while nursing
- For threatening abscesses or when the milk supply is abundant and the breast cannot be fully emptied with each feed
- Sudden, sharp pains in the breast and the back while feeding
- The nipples crack and this can become severe so quickly that they bleed

Pulsatilla
- Pains are felt in the small of the back and are better for gentle walking
- Experiences false ineffectual pains and the cervix does not dilate
- The pains are irregular and short or slow down, and are accompanied by a feeling of nausea and exhaustion
- A woman in a *Pulsatilla*-type labour becomes weepy, vulnerable and needs reassurance and tender care
- Very important remedy to turn the baby and to get the head to engage

Rhus tox
- Stretched ligaments cause restlessness and aching, dragging rheumatic pain in the small of the back, accompanied by stiffness
- Better for lying on a hard surface, for warmth, walking and movement, with the typical *Rhus tox* symptoms of being worse for initial movement and better for limbering up

Ruta
- Injuries to the tendons and ligaments
- It is also indicated for sore, bruised joint pains that are worse when lying on the relevant joints

Sepia
- An important constitutional remedy
- Used frequently by professional homoeopaths for pregnant and postpartum (following birth) symptoms
- It is suitable for extreme depletion and fatigue, postnatal baby blues and problems arising from hormonal changes

Urtica
- Helps to establish milk flow in the early days of breastfeeding
- Nipples cracked and sore

Miniature repertory for complaints pre- and postpartum

Abdominal pains or pains in the groin caused by a large or overactive baby: *Arnica, Bellis perennis*

Braxton Hicks contractions (see also Labour): *Belladonna, Caulophyllum, Chamomilla, Gelsemium, Pulsatilla*

Breasts (nursing complaints)
- **Breasts engorged:** *Belladonna, Bryonia, Phytolacca*

- **Milk insufficient:** *Urtica* (in potency or tincture)
- **Nipples cracked and sore:** *Calendula* cream, *Phytolacca*, *Silicea*

Breech position:
- **To turn baby:** *Pulsatilla*
- **Labour pains:** *Aconite, Arnica, Caulophyllum, Chamomilla, Gelsemium, Mag phos, Nat mur, Nux vom, Pulsatilla,* Rescue Remedy, *Sepia*

Constipation in pregnancy: *Nux vom, Pulsatilla*

Cramps in pregnancy: supplement with calcium and magnesium and use *Mag phos* and *Calc phos* in tissue salts

Cystitis: *Pulsatilla, Cantharis*

Drugged effect after labour as a result of medication taken: *Chamomilla, Nux vom*

Hair loss after childbirth: *Calc carb, Calc phos, Sepia* or *Silicea* in tissue salts

Indigestion and heartburn: *Bryonia, Nux vom, Pulsatilla*

Injuries during childbirth: *Arnica, Bellis perennis, Calendula, Hypericum*

Insomnia: *Aconite, Chamomilla, Ignatia, Nux vom, Pulsatilla*

Involuntary urination: *Pulsatilla*

Mastitis: *Belladonna, Phytolacca*

Mood changes:
- **Anticipatory anxiety:** *Argentum nit, Gelsemium*
- **Anxiety and fear:** *Aconite, Argentum nit*
- **Death, injury or abnormality of baby:** *Ignatia, Nat mur*

- **Depression and postnatal baby blues:** *Ignatia* (bleeding from emotional stress), *Nat mur*, *Pulsatilla*, *Sepia*
- **Irritable and angry:** *Chamomilla*, *Nux vom*
- **Irritable with husband, children and/or baby:** *Nux vom*, *Sepia*
- **Weepiness:** *Nux vom*, *Pulsatilla*

Nausea and morning sickness: *Ars alb*, *Ipecac*, *Nux vom*, *Pulsatilla*

Piles: *Ferrum phos*, *Hamamelis*, *Nux vom*

Stretching of uterine ligaments: *Bellis perennis*, *Bryonia*, *Rhus tox*, *Ruta*

HOMOEOPATHY *for* *your* PETS

'... cures on animals are the most appropriate and reliable.

The possible influences of imagination and diet,

which are often objected to, are with animals especially lacking.'

COUNT VON BOENNINGHAUSEN

Remember that this is first-aid treatment for uncomplicated cases. If the animal does not respond quickly or if it deteriorates, please seek help from a vet.

To administer the remedies, it is best to crush the dose and administer it directly on the animal's tongue. However, if this is impossible, as it often is with cats, conceal it in their food or in a treat. If all else fails, administer it in the drinking water.

Also remember to consult your ailments section and remedy pictures as the following are simple, basic suggestions. Animals respond well to 6ch, 12ch and 30ch potencies. Additional remedies have been mentioned in passing that have specific applications.

ABSCESSES
- For the very acute state with inflammation and great sensitivity to the slightest touch, give *Hepar sulph*.
- For chronic abscesses that must discharge pus to enable healing to take place, use *Silicea*.

ABRASIONS
- Wash area with a mixture of *Hypericum* and *Calendula* tincture diluted in water.

ANAL GLANDS
- Treat as for an abscess (*see* above).
- If the gland is already discharging heavily, use *Calc sulph*.

ANXIETY
- If the animal is fearful, trembling, excitable and difficult to control, or impulsive with a tendency to pass small amounts of urine frequently, has frequent stools or even diarrhoea, give it *Argentum nit* every one to four hours. Depending on whether the situation is ongoing or not, it will bring quick relief.

APPETITE
- If a lack of appetite is caused by a simple digestive problem such as a dietary indiscretion, for instance eating all your chocolates or something rotten in the garden, use *Nux vom*; if it is accompanied by excessive flatulence, use *Carbo veg*; or if it is caused from pining, think of *Ignatia*.

- For excessive or inappropriate appetite, that is eating chalk or stones, in fat animals, use *Calc carb* to regulate abnormal cravings and excessive hunger. In thin animals, *Calc phos* would be better indicated.

ARTHRITIS
- If the pain is worse from initial movement, but improves with continued exercise, that is the animal typically finds rising slow, difficult and painful but slowly 'limbers up', use *Rhus tox*.
- If the pain is worse from any motion, increases with further motion and the animal becomes irritable, wanting to lie on the painful part and be left undisturbed, then you are looking at a prescription of *Bryonia*.

BAD BREATH *(Halitosis)*
- Bad breath can be caused by gastric upset; *Nux vom* or *Carbo veg* will be useful, especially if the animal suffers from flatulence. Your animal may need deworming, need to have tartar removed from its teeth or have a decayed tooth removed – consult a vet. Give *Arnica* just prior to and after any dental work to encourage healing.

BITES
- All puncture wounds will benefit from a few doses of *Ledum*; bathe the surface of the wounds with *Hypericum* and *Calendula*.
- For stings from bees or wasps, *Apis* is very useful and can be given every 30 minutes to one hour until the pain settles.
- Apply *Urtica* tincture externally in undiluted form to help ease any allergic reactions.

BRUISES
- For superficial injury, bruising of any sort or after falls, *Arnica* is always indicated. If the bruise is deeper or more internal, *Bellis perennis* will be suitable.

BURNS
- For external use, dilute and apply compresses of *Urtica* tincture and give *Urtica* internally. For more severe burns, use *Cantharis* every two to four hours. depending on pain and severity. It would be useful to read the section on burns and their remedies (*see* page 124).

COLDS OR CAT FLU
- These often respond to *Ars alb*, given every three or four hours. If the animal does not improve quickly, consult a vet.

CONJUNCTIVITIS
see Eye inflammations, *see* opposite page

CONSTIPATION
- The most useful remedy is *Nux vom*. It is also important to look at the animal's diet.
- If the constipation is accompanied by much flatulence, *Carbo veg* can be useful.

COUGHS
Read the section on coughs (*see* page 137) and the indicated remedy pictures to see if you can get a closer 'fit' or 'match'.
- Hard, dry coughs often respond to *Phosphorus* every four hours.
- Coughs that stop when the animal is at rest respond well to *Bryonia*.

DIARRHOEA
If the animal does not respond quickly or its condition deteriorates, seek veterinary advice immediately.
- For watery stools with gastric complaints, vomiting and great weakness, give *Ars alb* after each stool or bout of vomiting.
- *Podophyllum* helps with watery, explosive stools.

EAR INFECTIONS
Refer to the section on ear infections (*see* page 148) and the remedy pictures as pets and children respond quite similarly to ear infections.
- When the animal is fretful, follows you around or there is a bland, thick discharge from the ear, use *Pulsatilla*.
- If there is great sensitivity to touch and an acutely painful and sensitive ear, consider *Hepar sulph*.
- Ears with a scabby, scaly surface or a discharge smelling of garlic require *Tellurium*.
- If ears suppurate and have an awful odour, and this happens more frequently at night, you will often need *Merc sol*.

ECZEMA

This very difficult condition usually requires the treatment of a vet. You may have to consider the animal's diet or allergies to fleas, washing powder or softeners in their bedding, or to their shampoo or dip. However, there are a few well-indicated remedies that you might like to try.

- For chilly, odorous animals, try *Psorinum* once daily for three days and wait. If there is no improvement, seek professional help.
- For warm-blooded animals seeking cool places like tile floors, and with a tendency to red, hot skins, give *Sulphur* once daily for three days and wait to see how they react. Only repeat the dose if there has been an improvement, or when the skin starts to deteriorate again.
- For dry skins tending to crack, *Petroleum* as a remedy is a consideration.
- If the eczema is scabby and has a wet, sticky discharge resembling honey, consider *Graphites* and give once daily for five days or until the condition starts improving. Repeat only when the eczema deteriorates.

EYE INFLAMMATIONS

- If it is mild and uncomplicated, try *Argentum nit* or *Euphrasia*. If the condition doesn't clear quickly, consult a vet.

GASTRITIS

Read the remedy pictures for the remedies mentioned below and refer to diarrhoea in the ailment section (*see* page 144).

- Vomiting with diarrhoea: *Ars alb*.
- Vomiting soon after food or drink is ingested: *Phosphoros*.
- With repeated vomiting: *Ipecac*.
- Also consider *Nux vom* and *Pulsatilla*.

HOMESICKNESS

- If an animal is pining in a boarding kennel, or if its owner is away from home or has died, *Ignatia* is indicated. If this does not bring speedy improvement, administer *Nat mur* daily or as needed.

MASTITIS
- If the mammary gland area is very hot, the indicated remedy is *Belladonna*. When the heat calms down, *Phytolacca* can be indicated.
- If the area of the mammary gland becomes hard, think of *Bryonia*. However, if the condition fails to heal and becomes chronic, *Silicea* three times a day should bring about resolution.
- For animals refusing to feed their offspring, *Sepia* given two or three times a day soon restores natural function.

NIPPLES
- For sore and cracked nipples, use *Graphites* three times a day and apply *Calendula* ointment or cream.

RHEUMATISM (*see also* **Arthritis**)
- For stiffness in general, or in some joints, especially in elderly dogs, *Causticum* given daily is a great help.
- In an acute state, *Ruta* every four hours is indicated, or if sprains don't heal, give *Ruta* once or twice a day.

RINGWORM
- If the lesions are more on your pet's body than head, *Tellurium* three times a day can be useful.
- Other remedies to consider are *Sepia* twice a day until the ringworm disappears or *Bacillinum* given daily for seven to 10 days.

SHOCK
- Use *Aconite* immediately after a great fright and follow instantly with *Arnica* or *Gelsemium* if the animal is trembling or almost paralyzed with weakness.
- Rescue Remedy is also of great benefit and can be administered freely.

TEETHING
- The main remedy for animals is *Chamomilla*, but the teething section under children's ailments (*see* page 126) will give you some good ideas for your pet if *Chamomilla* is not indicated.

VOMITING
- If it is caused by indigestible or bad food, consider *Ipecac*.
- For travel sickness with a strong tendency to vomit, *Cocculus ind* can be very helpful. Administer 30 minutes before a journey and frequently thereafter, or as needed.

WARTS
- *Thuja* once or twice a day until improvement begins, but not for longer than 10 days. *Thuja* tincture can also be applied locally at the same time as *Thuja* in potency is given internally.

WOUNDS
See also abrasions, bites, bruises, shock and sprains (under rheumatism)
- Injury to areas rich in nerve endings, for example the paws, tail and coccyx, respond very well to *Hypericum,* which should be repeated until the pain subsides and thereafter as needed.

REMEDY and AILMENT CARDS

'To serve a Higher Purpose, you need a healthy body as well as a healthy soul. How can you meditate, pray or study properly when the body's wellness is neglected? Take care of your body so that your soul can flourish.'

MENACHEM MENDEL SCHNEERSON

REMEDY CARDS

The user-friendly cards in this section have been designed to aid your memory and as a quick summary of the major points discussed under remedies and ailments. As mentioned before, it would be very useful to photocopy and laminate these cards and to keep them with your remedies and book for ease of reference.

ACONITE
- Fear, fright, shock
- Frightened, anxious, restless
- Fears the worst
- Suddenly ill
- Effects of cold, dry wind, draughts or getting chilled
- One cheek red and hot, the other cold and pale
- First stage of croup, colds, earaches, high fever as a result of chills

---

ALLIUM CEPA
- Increased discharge from nose, eyes and larynx
- Colds and hay fever
- Acrid nasal discharges with sneezing
- Burning, smarting or bland watering eyes (lacrimation)
- Sensitivity to light (photophobia)
- Colds from damp, cold weather
- Hacking cough from inhaling cold air

APIS
- Oedematous swelling, pink-red colour
- Urticaria and allergic reactions with oedema
- Pains burning, darting, stinging, better for cold
- No thirst
- Worse from all forms of heat
- Great sensitivity to touch

ARNICA

- Trauma and shock, physical and mental
- 'Leave me alone, there is nothing wrong with me'
- Injuries, falls, sprains, blows, bruises, fractures
- Sore, bruised sensation
- Altitude sickness
- Flu with sore, bruised muscles
- Effects of excessive heat
- Effects of overexertion, overwork, fatigue with aching

ARS ALB

- Anxiety and fear of being alone
- Physical and mental restlessness
- Ailments worse from midnight to 3 a.m.
- Chilliness
- Tidiness
- Burning pains and discharges which are better for warmth
- Great weakness and exhaustion, often from minor causes

BELLADONNA

- Sudden, violent onset of many ailments
- High fevers
- Bleeding, hot and gushing
- Intense heat of all inflamed parts
- Shiny, bright eyes, dilated pupils and sensitivity to light
- Illness starts at 3 p.m. or 3 a.m.
- Spasms and colic
- Use before there is pus formation
- Burning, inflammation, redness, dryness, sudden throbbing, pulsating pains

REMEDY *and* AILMENT CARDS

BRYONIA

- Worse for any motion
- Better from pressure
- Stitching, tearing pains
- Dryness of mucous membranes
- Irritability and desire to be left undisturbed
- Thirst for large quantities of liquid
- Slow onset of illness

CALENDULA

- Stops bleeding in tincture form
- Prevents suppuration and infection
- Promotes healing of open wounds and ulcers
- Takes pain out of injuries, tears, cuts and grazes

CANTHARIS

- Cystitis (inflammation of bladder)
- Violent, sudden onset of complaints
- Pain is burning, cutting and severe, and is accompanied by urination
- Skin complaints with large water blisters
- Skin reactions to burns and sunburn

CARBO VEG
- Collapse with desire to be fanned (corpse reviver)
- Extreme exhaustion from illness (has not been well since)
- Effects of shock, with collapse and fainting
- Needs air – must be fanned or have windows open
- Burning pains
- Sensitive to cold, cold to the touch with internal heat
- Bad effects of rich food, bad fish or meat, alcohol, carbon monoxide poisoning
- Flatulence and belching
- Distended, painful abdomen

CHAMOMILLA
- Bad temper, irritability, tantrums
- Effects of anger
- Pains seem unbearable
- One cheek hot and red, the other one cold and pale
- Wants to be carried and rocked
- Oversensitivity to touch, pain, to being spoken to or looked at
- Numbness with pain
- Teething

COLOCYNTHIS
- Cramping, twisting, grinding pains
- Very severe colic
- Pain is better when doubled up
- Pain much better for hard pressure
- For the ill-effects of anger, indignation, inflammation

EUPHRASIA

- Burning, acrid, watery, constant discharge from eyes
- Eyes sensitive to light (photophobia)
- Eyelids burning, red and swollen
- Colds and hay fever
- Bland, watery, nasal catarrh
- Loose cough during the day only, better from lying down
- Eye symptoms accompanying other illnesses

FERRUM PHOS

- For onset of fevers
- Slow onset of fever
- Symptoms less intense than *Belladonna*
- Flushed cheeks
- Nosebleeds

GELSEMIUM

- Drowsy, dull, dopey, shaky
- Anticipatory anxiety
- Effects of shock, bad news, etc.
- Viral infections and flu
- Usually no thirst
- Headaches from the neck upwards, like a band around the head

HEPAR SULPH
- Chilly, overreacts to draughts, cold
- Hypersensitive, irritable
- Pain is pricking, sharp or sticking like a splinter
- Better for warmth
- Croup better for steam
- Sweat profuse and offensive
- Suppuration, e.g. boils
- Catarrh

HYPERICUM
- Painfulness and sensitivity of the nerves
- Injury to nerves, especially fingers, toes, spine and brain
- Crush injuries
- Injuries to the tailbone
- Side effects of lumbar punctures and epidural anaesthetics
- Puncture or penetrating wounds, excessively sensitive
- Animal or insect bites

IGNATIA
- Sighing and yawning
- Hysterical outbursts
- Contradictory, paradoxical symptoms, changeable moods
- Physical ailments from emotional causes
- Likes to be alone to grieve silently
- Sympathy makes him feel worse
- Pain in small spots like a nail driven in
- *Globus hystericus* (sensation of a lump in the throat)
- Ailments from grief, strain, disappointed love, suppression of emotions

IPECAC
- Constant nausea, with a clean tongue
- Nausea accompanying complaints
- Nausea not better for vomiting
- Salivation with nausea
- Worse for thought or smell of food
- Sleepiness after vomiting
- Nosebleeds with cough and nausea
- Cough asthmatic, constricting and leading to gagging
- Sudden bronchitis with profuse, bubbly mucus, difficult breathing
- No thirst

KALI BICH
- Thick, yellow-green, stringy discharges
- Pain and infection in sinuses
- Postnasal discharges and crusts
- Pain felt in circumscribed small spots
- Pains changing location rapidly
- Croupy, metallic coughs
- Migraines with visual disturbances

LEDUM
- Puncture wounds
- Wounded parts are cold
- Coldness, better for cold applications
- Injury to eyes, often with haemorrhage
- Long-lasting discoloration after injury
- Animal and insect bites, and injuries from needles, splinters

MAG PHOS

- Neuralgic (nerve) pains, cramps and colic
- Better for warmth, bending, rubbing and passing wind

MERC SOL

- Hypersensitive to heat and cold
- Restlessness with trembling weakness
- Offensive breath, discharges and perspiration
- Night aggravations
- A continuing desire to pass urine or a stool
- Salivation and perspiration profuse, offensive and do not bring any relief
- Sore throat with flabby, slimy tongue, indented with tooth marks along the edge

NAT MUR

- Wants to be alone
- Ailments from grief
- Worse for consolation, but desires empathy
- Headaches hammering
- Worse at 10 a.m.
- Worse for sun and heat of sun
- Desire for salt, water, garlic and bitter substances
- Colds and hay fever

NUX VOM
- Irritability, impatience, stressed
- Nausea, heartburn, cramps
- Craves spices, fats, alcohol, coffee, tasty food
- Wakes at 3 a.m. with active, anxious mind
- Chilly
- Hunger with all ailments
- Sensitive to touch, pain, smell, noise, music, drugs, alcohol
- Frequent but ineffectual urge to vomit or to pass urine or a stool

PHOSPHORUS
- Needs sympathy, affection and company
- Anxious about his health
- Fears of the dark, ghosts, twilight, thunderstorms
- Burning pains
- Tends to bleed easily
- Weak, tight chest with coughs
- Desires ice cold drinks, ice cream, chocolate, salty and spicy foods
- Nausea and indigestion, better for cold drinks
- Palpitations with anxiety

PODOPHYLLUM
- Diarrhoea profuse, explosive, gushing, yellow-green or watery brown, painless, offensive
- Diarrhoea that accompanies teething
- Rumbling and gurgling before a stool

PULSATILLA

- Changeable symptoms and moods
- Moody, irritable, tearful, vulnerable
- Whining and clinging children
- Craves company, attention and consolation
- Discharges thick, yellow-green, bland
- Craves fresh air, sensitive to hot, stuffy rooms
- No thirst
- Better for moving around or being carried around slowly

RHUS TOX

- Extreme restlessness
- Worse for cold, damp weather
- Itchy, watery blisters like chicken pox
- Pain and stiffness with great need to move
- Pain from lifting heavy objects, sprains, strains
- Pain worse for rest, initial first movement and overexertion
- Pain better for continued movement and limbering up
- Flu with restless aches and pains

RUTA

- Sprains accompanied with weakness and slow healing
- Bruised, sore aching with restlessness
- Action on ankles, wrists, cartilage and tendons
- Ganglions, eyestrain
- Repetitive strain injuries
- Spot-pain at point where tendon attaches to bone
- Contraction of tendons
- Injuries to flexor muscles from lifting heavy objects

SILICEA

- Tonsils, abscesses and ear infections with pus
- Injuries and pussy sores healing slowly
- Expels foreign bodies, e.g. splinters
- Perspiration on hands, feet or head, and perspiration offensive
- Chilly, worse for any draught of air or chill, especially on head
- Head aches from neck to eyes
- Anxious, sensitive, weepy, needy, obstinate
- Fear of exams and public speaking

SPONGIA

- Dryness of mucous membranes
- Hacking, harsh, hollow, barking, dry, croupy coughs
- Croup, hoarseness and laryngitis
- Anxiety and difficulty in breathing
- Cough improved by drinking warm drinks or eating

SYMPHYTUM

- Injuries to bones, cartilage and periosteum
- Bone fractures
- Non-union of fractures
- Injuries to eyes from knocks, blows
- Ulcers on skin and in stomach

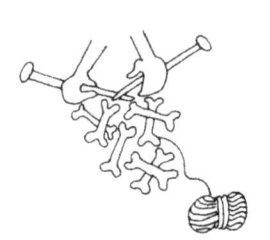

URTICA

- Urticaria (hives), bee stings
- Stinging, burning pains
- Effects of eating shellfish
- Gout and rheumatic attacks, often with urticaria
- Burns – apply locally in tincture and take internally in potency
- Promotes the production of breast milk

AILMENT CARDS

BITES

- *Apis* bee stings, swelling, shiny rosy red colour, urticaria, better for cold applications
- *Arnica* bruising, worse from slightest touch
- *Ledum* after insect bites, area surrounding the bite is cold, pale, swollen, better for cold applications, no bleeding
- *Silicea* promotes expulsion of sting, easy suppuration of wound
- *Staphysagria* severe itching changes location with scratching
- *Urtica* swollen, itchy bites, swelling, better for warmth

BLEEDING

- *Belladonna* blood is red with clots, gushing, feels warm, throbbing
- *Calendula* pure *Calendula* tincture dabbed onto dry cotton wool and applied with pressure to a wound stops bleeding (styptic)
- *Ferrum phos* flushes easily, pale and anaemic, nosebleeds, blood-streaked discharges
- *Ipecac* bright red, gushing, with nausea, no thirst
- *Phosphorus* persistent bleeding, small wounds bleed freely, accompanied by anxiety

BOILS
- *Apis* carbuncles with burning, stinging pain, swollen, rosy colour, better for cold
- *Arnica* small, frequent, recurrent crops, boils can be symmetrical
- *Ars alb* boils burning, better for warmth
- *Belladonna* rapid onset, throbbing, red, hot, inflamed
- *Hepar sulph* hypersensitive to touch, cold; splinter pain, better for warmth, offensive discharge
- *Merc sol* irregular, spreading, moist; pimples can occur around the main eruption
- *Silicea* sensitive to pressure, touch; better for warmth; hard lumps recur as boils

BURNS
- *Aconite* sunstroke, sunburn, with restlessness and fear
- *Cantharis* burns and scalds which blister, severe burning pain
- *Urtica* itching, stinging, burning pains, better for warmth

CHILDREN'S AILMENTS – TEETHING
- *Belladonna* dry mouth, red, swollen hot gums worse from cold applications, fever with dilated pupils, hot perspiration, pains come and go suddenly
- *Chamomilla* irritable, inconsolable, better carried, teething diarrhoea, one cheek pale and cold with the other red and hot
- *Nux vom* irritable, worse on waking, runny nose, sneezing, constipation
- *Podophyllum* teething diarrhoea, gushing and yellow
- *Pulsatilla* weepy and clingy, changeable moods, changeable stool, better moving around in fresh air, better for cold compress, no thirst

CHILDREN'S INFECTIOUS DISEASES

Chickenpox

- *Rhus tox* intense itching, with an eruption of water blisters, which feels better for warmth
- *Urtica* Use the tincture or cream on the spots to reduce itching

German measles (Rubella)

- *Belladonna* early stages of inflammation, red, flushed face, hot, dry red skin and mucous membranes, shiny eyes with dilated pupils, sensitivity to light, hot head with cold limbs
- *Merc sol* swollen lymph glands often starting at the base of the skull, feels hot one minute and cold the next, with sweating that does not alleviate the symptoms, the head feels as if it is full of cottonwool
- *Sulphur* red, itchy rash that feels worse for the warmth of a bed or a warm bath, appetite diminished but there is an increased thirst for room temperature drinks, desires sweets

Measles

- *Euphrasia* inflamed, sensitive eyes, profuse and bland discharge from nose, cough better for lying down, better from rest in bed
- *Pulsatilla* no thirst, chilly, desires fresh air, profuse, thick, yellow discharge from eyes, red rash, itching worse for warmth

Mumps
- *Merc sol* swollen glands in the neck are very painful and often worse at night,
- feels shivery, perspires heavily and is thirsty, but drinking liquids hurts swollen glands, bad breath with a sore throat
- *Pulsatilla* pain in the swollen glands is erratic and variable, feels weepy, wants sympathy and consolation, no thirst, swollen glands are accompanied by thick, yellow, bland mucus
- *Sulphur* swollen glands burn with pain, face and lips are red, feels very sleepy, more thirsty than hungry, but wants sweet drinks and foods, feels hot and wants to uncover herself

COLDS AND FLU
- *Aconite* from cold, dry winds; restless, anxious
- *Allium cepa* acrid nasal discharge, bland discharge from eyes, pain, hoarseness in voice-box, worse from warm room and in evening, better from open air, eyes red, burning and light-sensitive, hacking cough worse when inhaling cold air
- *Arnica* sore, bruised and weak feeling, bed feels hard, wants to be left alone, says nothing is wrong with him

COLDS AND FLU – continued
- *Ars alb* chilly, better from warm drinks and food, and warm applications, restless, weak, thirsty for sips of liquid, sits up to cough, frothy expectoration, fearful, wants company, burning discharges and watery colds, worse from midnight to 2 a.m., irritable, exacting, fastidious
- *Bryonia* worse for motion, thirst for large quantities of liquid, aching, stitching pains
- *Eupator perf* intense, aching, bone-breaking pains, backache, restless, chilly, throbbing headache (worse in occiput), aching eyeballs, vomits with nausea, laryngeal tickle, holds chest, thirsty

COLDS AND FLU – continued
- *Ferrum phos* flushed face, dry cough
- *Gelsemium* slow onset, aching body, heavy limbs, headaches in the back of the head with stiffness, flushed face with drooping eyelids, dull, confused, drowsy, trembling and weak, no thirst
- *Hepar sulph* chilly, hypersensitive, worse from dry, cold winds and draughts, perspires offensively, irritable, desires warm drinks, croupy cough improved by steam
- *Kali bich* wandering pains, pain at root of nose, discharges stringy, tough, lumpy or thick, hoarseness, laryngitis, worse from 2–4 a.m., blocked nose with watery, profuse nasal discharge, postnasal drip, sinusitis, brassy cough

COLDS AND FLU – continued
- *Nat mur* thick, white, clear, acrid discharges, worse for consolation or fuss, cold sores, hammering headaches, intense sneezing, alternate fluid and dry colds
- *Nux vom* worse from cold, dry, open air, wind and draughts, impatient, irritable, rawness in throat, nose blocked but water runs from it, violent sneezing and coughing, easily chilled, hungry
- *Pulsatilla* better from cold, fresh, open air, sitting up and gentle movement, worse from getting feet wet and from warmth, no thirst, chilly, weepy, discharges profuse, thick, bland, yellow or green, changeable symptoms

COLDS AND FLU – continued
- *Rhus tox* restless, aching flu, stiffness in the muscles and joints, chilly, pain worse from lying still and on first moving, feels better after loosening up, better from warm bath, rubbing, warm drinks and eating, urticaria with fever, desires cold milk, tongue coated, with triangular red tip, sore throat with swollen glands, can get flu from getting wet and laryngitis from air conditioning or cold winds

CRAMPS AND COLIC
- *Carbo veg* abdominal distress and colic, offensive gas, cannot bear tight clothing around waist, distension, pain forces the sick person to double up
- *Colocynthis* severe cramping pain, better for hard pressure, doubling up, warmth
- *Mag phos* great antispasmodic remedy, better from warmth and rubbing
- *Nux vom* cramping, worse from eating, drinking, motion, better from rest, sleep and heat

COUGHS
- *Aconite* dry, croupy, from cold wind, with fear at night
- *Ars alb* burning, tight, dry and wheezy, worse from midnight to 3 a.m., chilly, thirsty for sips, fearful
- *Belladonna* sudden, dry, barking, tickling cough, with sore throat, redness
- *Bryonia* dry, painful cough, holds chest and sides, headache with cough, stitching pains, worse for movement, better from lying on pain, great thirst
- *Drosera* paroxysmal bouts of dry, barking coughing, worse from lying down
- *Euphrasia* dry, hard cough and burning, watery eyes

COUGHS – continued
- *Ferrum phos* dry, hacking cough with some blood in the expectoration
- *Hepar sulph* from cold winds, croupy, hoarse, sweaty, chilly, better for steam
- *Ipecac* coughs with nausea, wheezing, constriction, vomiting, gagging, nosebleeds, clean tongue
- *Kali bich* thick, sticky, stringy, yellow-green mucus from nose and chest
- *Phosphorus* loose or dry, tickling cough, must sit up, anxiety, difficulty in breathing, wheezing, hacking, burning, hoarseness, colds to chest, mucus yellow-green

COUGHS – continued

- *Pulsatilla* catarrhal, loose during day, dry at night, no thirst, better for open air
- *Spongia* croup, hoarseness, laryngitis, dry, barking cough, better from drinking or eating

DIARRHOEA

- *Ars alb* watery, burning, offensive stools, weakness, anxiety, cutting pains
- *Chamomilla* foul, hot, green, offensive, slimy stools, mucus like chopped spinach, irritable
- *Merc sol* constant desire to pass stool, painful, ineffectual urging, never feels as if he has evacuated properly, green, slimy and foul, intense thirst, foul breath
- *Nux vom* from excesses, irritable, stools frequent, small evacuations, constant desire to pass stool, unease in rectum, cramps
- *Phosphorus* painless, copious, debilitating, involuntary diarrhoea, burning anus

DIARRHOEA – continued

- *Podophyllum* stools profuse, fetid, gushing, with gurgling, watery, undigested food and mucus, diarrhoea after eating or drinking, dentition
- *Pulsatilla* after eating fruit, ice cream and rich foods, differing stools, no thirst
- *Sulphur* drives you out of bed in early morning, red anus, burning pains

EAR INFECTIONS
- *Aconite* first stage, sudden onset from dry, cold winds, bright red ears, screams with pain, anxious, restless, burning thirst
- *Belladonna* sudden, burning fever, throbbing, in waves, external ear may be bright red, worse from any jarring motion
- *Chamomilla* teething, severe pain and irritability, redness of the cheek and ear, desires to be held and carried, soothed by warmth
- *Ferrum phos* pale red flush alternating with marked pallor, deafness and noises in the ear, early stages of a cold or sore throat

EAR INFECTIONS – continued
- *Hepar sulph* touchy, sweaty and chilly, sensitive to wind and cold air, stitching pain, boils in the ear canal, discharges, irritability
- *Merc sol* earache worse for warmth and at night, offensive perspiration, salivation, discharge yellow-green, pain in ears extends to teeth and glands beneath ear
- *Pulsatilla* changeable symptoms and moods, tearful, whining and clinging, discharges thick, yellow-green, no thirst, blocked ears, external ear red
- *Silicea* chilly, likes to lie on hot-water bottle, itching in Eustachian tubes, blocked ears 'pop' with yawning, mastoid pain

EMOTIONAL STATES – AILMENTS FROM:
- Abuse: *Ignatia, Staphysagria*
- Anticipation: *Argentum nit, Gelsemium, Silicea*
- Anxiety: *Aconite, Argentum nit, Gelsemium*
- Depression: *Iganatia, Nat mur, Pulsatilla*
- Fright: *Aconite, Arnica, Ars alb, Gelsemium*
- Grief: *Ignatia, Nat mur, Pulsatilla*
- Irritability: *Chamomilla, Nux vom*
- Overwork: *Arnica, Nux vom, Rhus tox, Silicea*
- Shock: *Aconite, Arnica, Gelsemium*
- Wounded pride: *Ignatia, Nat mur, Staphysagria*

EYE INFLAMMATIONS (CONJUNCTIVITIS)
- *Aconite* the '*Arnica*' of the eye, after any foreign body has entered eye, sudden, watering eyes, inflammation from exposure to cold, pain from ultra-bright glare
- *Allium cepa* bland tears and acrid nasal discharge, sensitive to light, burning eyelids with a desire to rub them, swelling around eyes, better in open air, hay fever
- *Apis* swelling of eyelids like water bags, hot tears, stinging pains, better from cool air and bathing, sensitive to light, worse for covering eyes
- *Ars alb* burning eyes, tears burn and mark the skin, swelling around eyes, red eyelids, better from external warmth, intense sensitivity to light

EYE INFLAMMATIONS (CONJUNCTIVITIS) – continued
- *Euphrasia* copious, acrid, watery or mucous tears, eyes dry 'as if there is sand in them', blinks a lot, can't bear bright light
- *Merc sol* discharge yellow-green and acrid, eyes pink and inflamed, worse at night and from warm bed, firelight, sunlight, glare, eyelids close spasmodically, with colds
- *Pulsatilla* after a cold, with thick, profuse, bland, yellow-green discharges, eyelids inflamed and stick together, better if cool, itches and burns, styes

EYE INJURIES
- *Aconite* wounds and foreign bodies in the eyes, for shock and fear
- *Arnica* injuries to the orbit and soft parts, bruising, haemorrhage of the conjunctiva
- *Ferrum phos* inflammation, red
- *Ledum* bruising with cold feeling in eye, better from cold applications
- *Symphytum* black eye due to blow of blunt object, surrounding tissue intact

REMEDY *and* AILMENT CARDS

FEVER

- *Aconite* cold, dry, after exposure to heat, sudden onset, restless, anxious, thirst for cold drinks
- *Ars alb* restless, anxious, worse from midnight to 3 a.m., chilly, frequent thirst for small quantities of liquid, burning pains
- *Belladonna* sudden, violent, red, hot, dry, inflammation, burning, often starts at 3 p.m.
- *Bryonia* worse for movement, better for pressure, thirst for large quantities of liquid, irritable

FEVER – continued

- *Chamomilla* Hypersenitive to pain, touch, with irritability, one cheek hot and red and other cheek pale, teething
- *Ferrum phos* fevers without intense symptoms, red cheeks
- *Gelsemium* dull, drowsy, dopey, dizzy, weakness, drooping, no thirst, chills up and down spine, aching, headaches
- *Ipecac* fevers with nausea or vomiting
- *Pulsatilla* no thirst with fever, changeable moods and symptoms, chilly but needs fresh air, weepy, whiny

FOOD POISONING

- *Ars alb* first remedy, with severe, simultaneous vomiting and diarrhoea, after midnight, weakness, restlessness, anxiety, chilly
- *Carbo veg* distension, flatulence and belching, chilly but wants air, 'gas bag'
- *Ipecac* constant nausea, no thirst, clean tongue, vomiting without relief
- *Nux vom* poisoning from excess food or drink, retching, constant urging to pass stools but stools small, cramping, desire to vomit
- *Urtica* shellfish poisoning with urticaria

HAY FEVER
- *Allium cepa* sneezing, acrid nasal discharge, bland tears
- *Apis* red, swelling membranes, bags under eyes
- *Ars alb* burning nasal discharge, better indoors
- *Euphrasia* burning discharge from eyes, bland discharge from nose, better from open air
- *Kali bich* feels like sinus, pressure at root of nose, stringy, yellow discharge
- *Nat mur* violent sneezing, watery discharge, fever blisters, better from washing face in cold water

HAY FEVER – continued
- *Nux vom* weak, chilly, hungry, nose blocked at night but runs during day, itching palate
- *Sabadilla* spasmodic, violent sneezing with copious watery discharge
- *Silicea* from effects of straw, with itching deep in ears

HEADACHE
- *Ars alb* midnight to 3 a.m., anxiety, restlessness, chilly but wants cold air
- *Belladonna* congestive, red face, throbbing, hammering, worse for noise, jarring and light, heatstroke
- *Bryonia* stitching or pressing pain, worse for slightest movement, better for pressure, thirst for large quantities of liquid
- *Carbo veg* headaches from overindulgence in rich foods and alcohol, worse from overheating, wants to be fanned
- *Gelsemium* heavy head, sensation of a band around head, visual disturbances, muscular soreness

HEADACHE – continued

- *Kali bich* pain in frontal sinuses and at root of nose, migraines with loss of vision, colds
- *Mag phos* better from pressure and external warmth
- *Nat mur* from grief, anxiety, visual disturbances with migraines, worse from sun
- *Nux vom* after indulgence in alcohol, rich food or coffee, chilly, worse from cold
- *Pulsatilla* from stuffy rooms, better walking in cool air, weepy

HEAT STROKE

- *Aconite* sudden, intense, anxiety, fear, shock, restless, panic, headaches, thirsty, shivering, strong pulse
- *Belladonna* intense, burning heat, dilated pupils, delirium, temperature high, strong pulse, throbbing pain, headache, skin intensely dry and hot, redness
- *Carbo veg* extreme weakness or collapse, need for air, feels hot inside
- *Gelsemium* weak, sleepy, dull, trembling, diarrhoea, no thirst, urination helps, drooping eyelids, weak pulse

HEAT STROKE – continued

- *Nat mur* blinding, throbbing headache, paleness, nausea, vomiting, thirsty, skin dry, burning, itching
- *Rhus tox* after exertion, with stiffness and restlessness, skin hot and itchy

INJURIES
- *Aconite* any injury with shock, fear, anxiety, restlessness, intense pain
- *Apis* stings, bites with rosy swelling, better for cold applications
- *Arnica* after accidents, strains, overuse, bruising of soft tissues
- *Bellis perennis* injuries to deep tissues, breasts, sprains and bruises
- *Calendula* antiseptic, stops bleeding
- *Cantharis* severe burns, sunburn
- *Hypericum* injuries to nerves, crushed fingertips, puncture wounds, shock, painful wounds

INJURIES – continued
- *Ledum* puncture wounds, stings, bites and bruises, better for cold applications
- *Rhus tox* sprains, lifting heavy objects, overexertion, injuries to tendons and joints, allergic rashes
- *Ruta* sprains to tendons, repetitive stress injuries, overstrain of eye muscles
- *Silicea* helps expel foreign bodies and splinters
- *Symphytum* injuries to tendons and bones, fractures that don't unite, black eyes
- *Urtica* burns, scalds, bleeding wounds, nosebleeds

MOUTH ULCERS
- *Ars alb* bluish ulcers, better for warmth
- *Hepar sulph* ulcers very sensitive to slightest touch, better warmth
- *Kali bich* punched out ulcers
- *Merc sol* ulcers with inflammation, swelling, salivation, better for cold, offensive mouth and breath
- *Nat mur* ulcers and vesicles, dry mouth, mapped tongue

SHOCK
- *Aconite* after acute shock or fright, anxious, restless, fears death, intense thirst
- *Arnica* after traumatic injuries, says there is nothing the matter with him, fears touch, bed feels too hard, sore, weak, bruised feeling
- *Carbo veg* physical collapse, wants to be fanned
- *Gelsemium* wants to be held, shakes, weak with heaviness in all the limbs, needs a drink, weak at the knees, dizzy and drowsy
- *Ignatia* emotional shocks like sad events, grief, mourning, accidents and disappointments, and for nervous conditions of emotional origin, hypersensitivity with sighing, fainting, sobbing, desires to be alone, contradictory symptoms

SINUSITIS AND CATARRH
- *Hepar sulph* facial bones worse from slightest touch, cold, pain at root of nose, sneezes in cold wind, nose blocked, postnasal drip, aids discharge
- *Kali bich* pressure, fullness, pain at root of nose, headache improved by nose running, pain in small spots, no smell, discharge thick, stringy, sticky, greenish-yellow, postnasal drip, crusts, nose blocked with violent sneezing
- *Merc sol* pain extends from sinuses to teeth, discharge bloody, yellow-green, sneezes in sunshine

SINUSITIS AND CATARRH – continued
- *Nat mur* violent, watery cold with violent and rapid onset of sneezing, blocked nose, discharge like raw white of egg, inflammation in frontal sinuses, dry sinusitis, tearing pain
- *Pulsatilla* one nostril blocked, pain to teeth
- *Silicea* headache in forehead, itching nose, itching in Eustachian tubes, sneezing, hard crusts, discharges infected, dizziness worse looking up, wants warmth to the head, pain better from pressure, chilly

SORE THROATS

- *Apis* swollen, uvula swollen, bright pinky-red, better from cold, no thirst, burning, stinging pain
- *Belladonna* throbbing, burning, red, dry, inflamed, sudden onset at 3 p.m., fever
- *Hepar sulph* splinter pain extends to ears, better for warm drinks, with chilliness, perspiration and irritability
- *Kali bich* swollen uvula, stringy mucus, ulcers, better from warm drinks
- *Merc sol* slimy, better from cold drinks, salivation, swollen glands, indented flabby tongue, sweating, sensitive to heat and cold, offensive breath, sometimes with pus

SORE THROATS – continued

- *Nux vom* raw, rough, tight, extends to ears, itching in Eustachian tubes, with colds, irritable, hungry
- *Silicea* pus formation, swollen glands, lingering conditions, chilly, sweaty head and feet

URTICARIA

- *Apis* from stings, rosy-red, better from cold, swelling locally
- *Nat mur* worse after exertion or being heated
- *Rhus tox* itching eruptions from contact with some plants, better from heat
- *Urtica* from shellfish, prickling heat and itching, better from warmth

QUESTIONS
and ANSWERS

'Aude spera – Dare to know'

SAMUEL HAHNEMANN

All the remedies that are the answers to these questions are found in this book.

Questions

1. Name a remedy for a dry, hard cough that is painful whenever the sick person coughs. The pain is often felt under the breastbone and any exertion seems to make the cough worse. He feels very thirsty for numerous glasses of water at a time.

2. Describe a remedy for a person suffering from food poisoning. He wakes in the early hours of the morning with vomiting and diarrhoea, and feels faint. Even the thought of food can set off further retching. As he is worried about his condition, he does not want to be left alone. He needs ...

3. This remedy will cure a person with constant nausea. Her saliva flows excessively and her tongue is clean and uncoated.

4. Cutting away or burning off warts is frowned on in homoeopathic practice because
   a) they leave unsightly scars
   b) more warts will grow
   c) the vital force in the person's body is 'suppressed' and the chronic disease can be driven from the skin level to a deeper internal level of the body
   d) all of the above.

5. Six-year-old Janet is tearful, feels vulnerable and doesn't want to go to school and leave her mother. She has a cold with thick, yellow-green mucus pouring from her nose and cries at the slightest thing. She whines and complains that her ear is getting sore. Her appetite and thirst are diminished. She needs ...

6. A man sneezes constantly and complains of a pouring cold with a clear nasal discharge that burns his upper lip, leaving it red and sore. Even his reddened eyes pour out liquid. He wants the windows open for fresh air, but that makes him cough more. His cold and sneezing will quickly be relieved by ...

7. *Euphrasia* has a loose cough during the day, with profuse expectoration that is better for lying down. *Phosphorus*, on the other hand, has a cough that:
   a) is dry, hard, barking and worse while standing
   b) is loose and deep, and worse while lying down so that the sick person needs to sleep propped up with many pillows
   c) chirrups like a cricket while bathing
   d) sounds like a log being sawn and is accompanied by croup

8. Father's sinusitis has started up again and he has become as irritable as a bear with a sore head. He has been walking around with a scarf around his neck and a cap on. He shouts if we leave the windows open and he feels the slightest draught. He says his whole head is bruised, sore and blocked. Mother had better give him ...

9. Just before the child became ill, he had bad breath and his mother noticed that he was dribbling a lot more than usual. 'I guess he is teething again', she said, 'but even his sweat smells unpleasant'. After a day of being miserable and feeling uncomfortably hot, he started suffering from a sore throat and a sore ear. The glands in his throat and just below his ear were larger than usual and his mother also noticed that his tongue was coated and flabby. He needs ...

10. Abi hurt her back from lifting a heavy box incorrectly. The pain feels better when she walks around but much worse after sitting still and then starting to move again. She wants a hot-water bottle on her back and wants to lie on a hard floor. By taking ... her back will be better by the morning.

11. Jane is very moody after her boyfriend has dropped her for someone who is 'really cool'. She weeps hysterically alone in her room and walks around sighing and saying that her parents don't understand her. She laughs and cries alternately. She needs ... to restore her calm and give her more perspective.

12. Belinda gets a migraine that starts with flickering spots in front of her eyes that lead to a hammering, bad headache. This happens every year on the anniversary of her mother's death. She needs ... for the headache and to help her resolve the grief that she has tried to put behind her.

13. Anxiety before an exam and a fear of going blank.

14. Anxiety with fear and restlessness from a shock.

15. Weeping, wants consolation and company, feels vulnerable and has no thirst.

16. A feeling of injustice – 'it's just not fair'.

17. A remedy for thick yellow-green strings of mucus from the nose or from a sinus infection?

18. Fear of failure, but then does very well. Perfectionist, lacks confidence in herself.

19. Intense irritability and impatience from stress or being premenstrual. Wants everything to be done properly.

20. Irritability with hypersensitivity to pain. This remedy is often used for teething babies.

21. Anxiety, often worse in the middle of the night, accompanied by a fear of death and nervous pacing. Perfectionist and critical. Wants company and reassurance.

22. Anxiety and rushing around. Fear becomes so intense that the sick person won't walk on the cracks of the pavement or go into narrow lifts.

23. Teething baby with yellow, gushing diarrhoea at 4 a.m.

24. Flu with aching muscles and stiffness of the joints that feels worse when the sick person lies in bed too long. He feels better after walking around for a little while and after a hot bath. He feels like drinking milk, and the tip of his tongue is red. The remedy needed for this is ...

25. For a headache caused by a hangover, and accompanied by irritability and hypersensitivity to noise and light, consider using ...

26. Name a remedy that is useful for severe cramping pains in the stomach and where the sick person feels better from a hot-water bottle and doubling up.

27. After Mary had a dreadful car accident and broke her arm and her leg, she kept insisting that she was 'fine' and wanted to go home. While waiting for the ambulance, I frequently gave her ...

28. A remedy for heatstroke with flushed, burning, hot, red face, dilated pupils and a throbbing headache is ...

29. My back went 'out' when I tried to lift and move the fridge to spring-clean. It feels weak and is definitely better for movement but worse if I lie on the sore part. I tried *Rhus tox* but it didn't help much. What should I try next?

30. Johnny came home from school crying as he had a very sore tailbone – his friends had pulled the chair out from under him as he was about to sit down. He fell hard onto his coccyx. Johnny's mother gave him ... for the nerve pain.

Answers

1. *Bryonia*	11. *Ignatia*	21. *Ars alb*
2. *Ars alb*	12. *Nat mur*	22. *Argentum nit*
3. *Ipecac*	13. *Gelsemium*	23. *Podophyllum*
4. D – all of the above	14. *Aconite*	24. *Rhus tox*
5. *Pulsatilla*	15. *Pulsatilla*	25. *Nux vom*
6. *Allium cepa*	16. *Staphysagria*	26. *Mag phos*
7. B	17. *Kali bich*	27. *Arnica*
8. *Hepar sulph*	18. *Silicea*	28. *Belladonna*
9. *Merc sol*	19. *Nux vom*	29. *Ruta*
10. *Rhus tox*	20. *Chamomilla*	30. *Hypericum*

GLOSSARY

Acute diseases
Diseases that are self-limiting, that is they have a beginning or incubation stage, a middle stage of symptoms, and a convalescent phase at the end.

Aggravation
A very temporary worsening of symptoms. This sometimes follows taking a remedy but is usually and quickly succeeded by a distinct improvement in the sick person's condition.

Allopathy
Term loosely applied to conventional medicine.

Antidote
A remedy taken to counteract, or stop certain symptoms.

Biological reaction
The reaction of the living organism to external or internal stress.

Chronic diseases
Deep-seated diseases that are not self-limiting. These diseases develop slowly and unpredictably, and sick people are not able to eradicate the illnesses by themselves.

Clinical picture
The presenting pathological or functional disorder, or existing disease syndrome, named according to conventional medicine.

Complete symptom
Causation – what caused it?
Location – where is it?
Nature of sensation – what does it feels like?
Modalities – what makes it better or worse?
Concomitant – what else occurred at the same time?

Concomitant

A symptom that is far removed from the main illness picture, but occurs at the same time as the problem.

Constitutional remedy

A remedy prescribed on the basis of the temperament, character and general reaction of the sick person (his constitutional type) as well as the local symptoms of the disease. This is the work of a professional homoeopath.

Doctrine of Signatures

The manner in which the substance appears, grows or behaves, and so on, will give you an indication of its potential in illness. An example of this is the lungwort plant which has leaves that resemble lungs.

Drug picture

A summary of the symptoms, mental states and disorders that a substance is capable of causing (and healing) in living organisms, that is via the Law of Similars (*see also* Clinical picture).

General symptoms

Symptoms prefaced by 'I' and relating to the whole being, for example 'I' like heat, 'I' love sweets, and so on.

Holistic

The concept of totality in the sick person and in the remedy. It means seeing the sick person in every aspect of his mental and physical functioning, and embracing the individuality of the sick person in his problem, that is non-splintering of the symptom presentation. The whole is always more than its parts.

Homoeopathy

The system of medicine developed by Samuel Hahnemann, invoking the principle that effective and non-toxic treatment may be given by using substances that can cause symptoms in the healthy person that will be similar to those from which the sick person is suffering. This is summarized as *Similia simillibus curentur* (Like cures like). *See also* Law of Similars.

Incompatible
Not agreeing with.

Keynote symptom
see Key symptom.

Key symptom
Symptom corresponding to the leading symptom of the remedy and/or sick person – complete and characteristic.

Law of Similars
The treatment using similars is best expressed by homoeopathy's motto – Like cures like (*Similia simillibus curentur*). In other words, the application of the Law of Similars means that the remedy for any individual illness is the very substance that can produce a similar symptom picture and pattern of the illness in a healthy person.

Local symptoms
Symptoms pertaining to the part, organ or function – the 'my' symptoms, for example 'my' stomach, 'my' hair, 'my' head.

Materia medica
Describes signs and symptoms of remedies, and makes up the homoeopathic pharmacopoeia – a list of remedies and their associated symptoms and use.

Mentals
Symptoms of the intellect and emotions.

Modality
Those factors that qualify a particular symptom, for example pain worse from motion (aggravated) or better from local heat (alleviated by).

Objective symptoms
Symptoms that can be verified by the observer, for example fever.

Particular symptoms
see Local symptoms

Polycrests
Remedies which have multipurpose uses.

Potency
Highly diluted, energized substance prepared according to specified and standardized pharmaceutical methods. Soluble substances are put through the process of serial dilution and succussion (or trituration if insoluble) at each stage of dilution according to homoeopathic methodology and scales.

Proving
The testing of substances on healthy volunteers (provers) who take repeated doses and record in detail any symptoms produced. These proving symptoms give us the homoeopathic Materia medica.

Signs
Objective symptoms.

Simillimum
The single remedy that best fits the total symptom picture. *Similia simillibus curentur* – Like cures like.

Symptoms of the sick person
Change of conditions from health to illness that show the body's reaction and call for treatment.

Symptoms of the remedy
Conditions and symptoms produced by 'proving' the remedy, that is giving it to healthy provers and recording the symptoms they produce.

Subjective symptoms
Symptoms the sick person experiences not verifiable by an observer.

Succussion
Violent shaking at each stage of dilution, for a specified time, in the preparation of a potency.

Tincture
Herbal tincture (not a potency) made by extracting the herb in an alcohol and water mixture as defined in a pharmacopoeia.

Trituration
The process of mixing a substance in a mortar and pestle with lactose powder for a prolonged period of time.

Vital force
The innate recuperative or balancing power within the human body, which can be stimulated by a homoeopathic potency. In disease, the remedy can help the vital force to revert to self-regulation.

Vitalism
The doctrine that holds that there is a vital principle. Theory holding that underlying all vital phenomena there is a life-giving, life-preserving, life-directing and integrating force in every living organism (Harald Gaier).

BIBLIOGRAPHY

We have selected some books you might want to read to broaden your knowledge and for your general interest. Enjoy!

Blackie, Margery G. *The Patient, not the Cure*. Macdonald and Jane's, London, 1976.

Brewster O'Reilly, Wenda (editor). *Dr Samuel Hahnemann Organon of the Medical Art*. Birdcage Books, Washington, USA, 1996.

Castro, Miranda. *Complete Homeopathic Handbook*. Pan MacMillan, London, 1996.

Castro, Miranda. *Homeopathy for Pregnancy, Birth and Your Baby's First Year.* St Martin's Press, New York, 1993.

Cook, Trevor M. *Samuel Hahnemann – The Founder of Homoeopathic Medicine.* Thorsons Publishers Ltd., Wellingborough, Northamptonshire, 1981.

Cummings, Stephen and Ullman, Dana. *Everybody's Guide to Homeopathic Medicine.* Victor Gollancz Ltd, Great Britain, 1986.

Dhama and Dhama. *Homoeopathy – the Complete Handbook.* UBS Publishers, Distributors Ltd, New Delhi.

Gaier, Harald. *Thorsons Encyclopaedic Dictionary of Homoeopathy.* Thorsons Publishers Ltd., Wellingborough, Northamptonshire, 1991.

Handley, Rima. *A Homeopathic Love Story – The Story of Samuel and Melanie Hahnemann.* North Atlantic Books, Berkley, California, 1990.

Horvilleur, Alain. *The Family Guide to Homeopathy.* Health and Homeopathy Publishing Inc., Virginia, 1979.

Kent, J.T. *Lectures on Homoeopathic Materia Medica.* B Jain. S Dey. Calcutta. 1911, reprinted 1962.

Koehler, Gerhard. *The Handbook of Homeopathy – Its Principles and Practice.* Thorsons Publishers Limited. Ltd., Wellingborough, Northamptonshire, 1983.

Kruzel, Thomas. *The Homeopathic Emergency Guide.* North Atlantic Books, Berkley, California, 1992.

Lockie, Dr Andrew. *The Family Guide to Homeopathy – The Safe Form of Medicine for the Future.* Elm Tree Books, London,1989.

Subotnik, Steven. *Sports and Exercise Injuries.* North Atlantic Books, Berkley, California, 1991.

Tyler, Margaret *Homoeopathic Drug Pictures*. Health Science Press, England, 1970.

Ullman, Dana. *Homeopathic Medicine for Children and Infants*. Piatkus, California, 1992.

Vithoulkas, George. *A New Model for Health and Disease*. North Atlantic Books, Berkley, California, 1991.

A few herbal books used in writing this book:

Hoffmann, David. *The Holistic Herbal Way to successful Stress Control*. Thorsons Publishers Limited. Ltd., Wellingborough, Northamptonshire, 1986.

Howarth, Dr Bessie. *Herbal Healing Inheritance*. Regency Press (London & New York), 1989.

Roberts, Margaret. *Herbs for Healing*. Woolworths. Jonathan Ball Johannesburg for Woolworths,1989.

Mills, Simon Y. M.A., M.N.I.M. *The Dictionary of Modern Herbalism*. H Healing Arts Press, Rochester, Vermont, 1988.

Pizzorno Jr, Joseph E, Murray, Michael T and Joiner-Bey, Herb. *The Clinician's Handbook of Natural Medicine*. Harcourt Health Sciences, Churchill Livingstone, London, 2002.

INDEX

Bold page numbers indicate main entries

A

Abrasions *see* Injuries
Abscess, dental 103
Aconite 8, 31, **42–3**, 51, 66, 70, 104, 113, 124, 132, 138, 148–9, 152, 158, 160, 162, 174, 177, 184, 195, 202, 210
Allergy 26, 28, 35, 45, 46, 47, 51, 64, 65, 96, 97, 107, 157, 167, 179, 186, 189, 193
Allium cepa **44–5**, 64, 132, 158, 168
Anaemia 35, 38
Anxiety *see* Emotional states
Apis **45–7**, 116, 117, 122, 125, 158, 168, 177, 189–90, 193
Argentum nit 152–3, 202, 206, 209
Arnica 32, **47–9**, 100, 105, 106, 114, 117, 122, 153, 160, 161, 177–8, 184, 198, 201, 202, 207, 210
Ars alb 46, **49–51**, 88, 122, 132–3, 138, 145, 153, 158, 162–3, 165, 168, 171, 181, 203, 208, 209
Arthritis 55, 97, 107, 195
Asthma 34,35, 51, 75, 76, 139, 141

B

Back injuries *see* Injuries
Belladonna 7, 30, **51–3**, 66, 97, 102, 119, 121, 122, 126, 128, 138, 148, 149, 163, 171, 175, 190, 195, 198, 201, 210
Bellis perennis 178, 198, 201, 202, 203, 207
Bites 47, 72, 80, 107, **116–8**, 177, 178, 179, 180, 193
Bladder infections 57, 58, 83, 84, 110, 144, 202
Bleeding 43, 48, 49, 52, 53, 55, 56, 59, 63, 66, 67, 76, 89, 90, 91, 110, **118–21**, 177, 178, 179, 180, 181, 182
Boils 34, 47, 49, 52, 53, 70, 71, 102, 103, **121–3**, 150
Breasts *see* Women's ailments
Bronchitis *see* Chest infections
Bruising *see* Injuries
Bryonia 9, 25, 31, **53–5**, 98, 133, 138, 163, 171, 201, 202, 203, 207, 208, 210
Burns 47, 56, 57, 58, 107, 110, **124–5**, 178, 180

C

Calc carb 37, 202, 207
Calc fluor 196
Calc phos 196, 202, 207
Calendula 47, **55–6**, 114, 119, 120, 121, 123, 161, 178, 183, 192, 202, 206, 207, 210
Cantharis **58–60**, 107, 124, 178, 207
Carbo veg **58–60**, 142, 166, 172, 175, 184, 206, 207, 208
Catarrh *see* Sinusitis and Catarrh
Caulophyllum 199, 201, 202
Chamomilla 32, 43, **60–2**, 70, 76, 126, 145, 149, 153, 163, 195, 201, 202, 203, 210
Chest infections 76, 83, 84, 89, 90, 91, 191, 199
Chicken pox *see* Children's infectious diseases
Childbirth *see* Women's ailments
Children's infectious diseases **127–31**
  Chicken pox 33, 98, **127–8**
  German measles **128–9**
  Measles 47, 64, 65, 95, **129**, 131
  Mumps 84, **130**, 131, 150
Cimicifuga racemosa 195, 199
Colds and Flu 9, 26, 33, 43, 44, 45, 47, 50, 51, 55, 55, 63, 64, 65, 67, 68, 69, 71, 79, 83, 85, 86, 88, 91, 92, 94, 95, 96, 98, 104, **131–7**, 140, 141, 149, 170, 172, 186, 189
Colic *see* Cramps and Colic
Colocynthis **62–3**, 81, 82, 142–3, 153
Colon, spastic *see* Digestive disorders, Irritable bowel syndrome
Concussion *see* Injuries
Conjunctivitis *see* Eye inflammations
Constipation 89, 126, 143, 171
  see also Women's ailments, Pregnancy
Coughs 6, 33, 42, 43, 44, 51, 52, 54, 55, 64, 65, 66, 70, 71, 74, 75, 76, 78, 79, 90, 91, 94, 98, 103, 104, 105, 106, 113, 129, 132, 133, 134, 135, 136, **137–41**, 163, 168
Cramps and Colic 52, 53, 60, 61, 62, 63, 74, 75, 81, 87, 89, **142–4**, 145, 146, 153, 167
Croup *see* Coughs
Cystitis *see* Bladder infections

D

Dehydration 51, 58, 59, 93, 110, 144, 145, 148, 165, 167, 174, 176
Dentition *see* Teething
Depression *see* Emotional states
Diarrhoea *see* Digestive disorders
Digestive disorders
  Burping 59, 60, 94, 166, 175
  Diarrhoea 28, 32, 43, 50, 51, 58, 60, 62, 68, 83, 84, 90, 91, 92, 93, 94, 95, 110, 118, 120, 126, 142, **144–8**, 153, 154, 165, 166, 175
  Distension 59, 60, 142, 143, 166
  Flatulence 142, 143, 144, 146, 153, 166, 175

INDEX 253

Food poisoning 32, 33, 50, 51, 59, 144, 145, 147, **165–7**
Heartburn and Indigestion 87, 89, 91, 153, 166
Irritable bowel syndrome 34, 144
Nausea 50, 62, 75, 76, 87, 89, 90, 91, 133, 136, 139, 142, 145, 164, 166, 167, 170, 176
Vomiting 50, 51, 58, 62, 75, 76, 77, 88, 88, 90, 94, 111, 119, 142, 145, 146, 147, 164, 165, 166, 167, 170, 176
Dioscorea 195
Distention *see* Digestive disorders
Dizziness 54, 67, 185, 188
 see also Vertigo
Dong quai (Angelica sinensis) 195
Drosera rotundifolia 6, 138–9
Drowsiness 67, 68, 134, 164, 170, 185

E

Earache and Ear infections 43, 44, 52, 53, 62, 66, 67, 71, 79, 84, 95, 101, 102, 103, 126, **148–51**, 191
Echinacea 123, 127, 136, 151, 164, 192, 194
Eczema *see* Skin disorders
Emotional states **152–7**
 Ailments from abuse 42, 155
 Ailments from anticipation 68, 152, 153, 154
 Ailments from anxiety 42, 43, 46, 49, 51, 68, 69, 87, 91, 101, 102, 103, 104, 116, 124, 132, 145, 149, 152, 153, 154, 155, **156–7**, 162, 165, 171, 172, 174, 177, 184, 195
 Ailments from depression 34, 36, 72, 154, 155, **157**, 195
 Ailments from disappointed love 73, 75, 154
 Ailments from drugs, coffee 62, 173

 Ailments from fright 42, 43, 68, 69, 74, 152, 153, 154, 155, 184
 Ailments from grief 73, 74, 75, 85, 86, 135, 143, 154, 184, 185
 Ailments from humiliation and wounded pride 6, 63, 75, 143, 153
 Ailments from hysteria 73, 74, 154, 183
 Ailments from/with irritability 25, 32, 54, 60, 63, 69, 70, 83, 87, 88, 131, 133, 135, 143, 146, 149, 150, 153, 154, 155, 163, 166, 169, 190, 191
 Ailments from overwork 69, 87, 153
 Ailments from restlessness 42, 46, 49, 50, 51, 52, 63, 82, 83, 96, 98, 99, 100, 124, 132, 143, 145, 146, 149, 152, 153, 162, 165, 171, 174, 175, 176, 177, 179, 184, 191
 Ailments from shock 42, 43, 47, 48, 49, 58, 60, 68, 69, 114, 152, 153, 154, 174, 179, 183–5
 Ailments from/with weepy moods 7, 26, 30, 46, 93, 95, 130, 136, 155, 164, 173, 185
Eupatorium perfoliatum 133
Euphrasia **64–5**, 129, 132, 139, 158, 159, 168, 209
Eye inflammations 44, 46, 64, 65, 83, 84, 95, 129, **157–9**, 177
Eye injuries 43, 47, 49, 80, 105, 106, 111, **160–1**, 179, 180
Eye strain 99, 100, 159, 170, 179
Eye styes 34, 47, 71, 159
Exertion, effects of 47, 48, 49, 96, 98, 176, 179

F

Fainting 54, 58, 60, 166, 184, 185
Ferrum phos **65–7**, 119–20, 121, 132, 134, 139, 149, 160, 163, 203

Fever 42, 43, 51, 52, 53, 62, 67, 83, 84, 110, 111, 121, 126, 128, 129, 131, 136, 148, **162–5**, 171, 186, 190
Flatulence *see* Digestive disorders
Flu *see* Colds and Flu
Food poisoning *see* Digestive disorders
Fractures *see* Injuries

G

Ganglion 99, 100
Gelsemium 31, **67–9**, 102, 114, 124, 134, 153–4, 164, 171, 172, 175, 184–5, 199–200, 201, 202, 210
Glands, swollen 83, 84, 111, 128, 130, 136, 150, 191, 192
Gout 107

H

Haemorrhoids 89, 120
Halitosis 83, 182, 191
Hangovers 89
Hay fever 35, 44, 45, 47, 51, 64, 65, 79, 85, 86, 88, 89, 103, **167–70**, 172
Headaches 25, 26, 51, 52, 53, 54, 55, 66, 67, 68, 69, 74, 78, 79, 81, 85, 86, 87, 92, 95, 97, 101, 102, 111, 132, 133, 134, 135, 138, 154, 164, 168, **170–4**, 174, 176, 186, 187, 188, 195
Heartburn *see* Digestive disorders
Heatstroke **174–6**
Hepar sulph 32, 50, **69–71**, 102, 104, 113, 123, 134, 139, 150, 182, 186, 190, 192, 206, 208
Herpes 98
Hypericum 32, **71–3**, 114, 178–9, 202, 206, 207, 211

I

Ignatia 31, **73–5**, 85, 154, 185, 195, 202, 203, 206, 209
Impetigo *see* Skin disorders
Indigestion *see* Digestive disorders

Infection, general 55, 56, 57, 128, 177, 186, 189
Inflammation 51, 53, 62, 66, 67, 83, 91, 102, 121, 128, 163, 167, 182, 190
Injuries **176–81**
   Abrasions 56
   Back injuries 72, 96, 97, 98, 100, 106, 178, 179, 180
   Bruising 47, 48, 49, 66, 80, 99, 100, 110, 117, 177, 178, 179, 181
   Childbirth, during *see* Women's ailments, Pregnancy
   Concussion 72, 73, 110, 170, 178, 180
   Fractures 47, 49, 55, 100, 105, 106, 179, 180
   Injuries to bones 99, 100, 105, 106, 114, 179
   Injuries to breast tissue 178
   Injuries to joints 98, 100
   Injuries to ligaments, tendons and cartilage 32, 55, 98, 99, 100, 105, 106, 179
   Injuries to muscle 98, 99
   Injuries to nerves 32, 72, 114, 178
   Injuries to small joints 100
   Injuries to soft tissue 32, 56, 114, 178
   Neuralgia 62, 63, 72, 81
   Nosebleeds 43, 52, 56, 60, 66, 76, 90, 91, 119, 120, 132, 139, 163, 180, 187
   Puncture wounds 55, 56, 71, 72, 80, 111, 114, 177, 178, 179, 180
   Splinters 80, 101, 103, 179
   Sprains and Strains 47, 49, 55, 72, 98, 99, 100, 105, 178
Insect bites *see* Bites
Insomnia 43, 60, 75, 85, 89, 155, 194, 195
Ipecac 43, **75–7**, 120, 121, 139, 164, 166, 203, 209, 211
Itching 45, 96, 97, 107, 116, 117, 125, 128, 167, 188, 191, 193, 194 *see also* Urticaria

J
Joints *see* Injuries

K
Kali bich **77–9**, 113, 134–5, 140, 168–9, 172, 182, 187, 191

L
Laryngitis 43, 45, 53, 78, 90, 91, 104, 105, 134, 136, 141
Ledum **79–80**, 106, 116, 117, 161, 179, 207
Ligaments, tendons and cartilage *see* Injuries

M
Mag phos **81–2**, 102, 143, 172, 202
Measles *see* Children's infectious diseases
Meningitis 69
Menopause *see* Women's ailments
Menses (menstruation) *see* Women's ailments
Merc sol 57, **82–4**, 89, 123, 128, 130, 140, 145–6, 150, 159, 182, 187, 191, 208
Migraines *see* Headaches
Mouth ulcers and dental problems 62, 72, 81, 170, **181–3**
Mucous *see* Sinusitis and Catarrh
Mumps *see* Children's infectious diseases
Muscle *see* Injuries

N
Nausea *see* Digestive disorders
Nat mur **84–6**, 135, 154, 169, 172, 176, 182, 187, 193, 200, 202, 203, 209
Neuralgia *see* Injuries
Nosebleeds *see* Injuries
Nux vom 32, **86–9**, 126, 135, 143, 146, 154–5, 166–7, 169, 173, 191, 195, 200, 202, 203, 207, 208, 209

P
Pain 7, 25, 30, 32, 49, 54, 57, 58, 60, 62, 63, 72, 74, 81, 96, 102, 110, 116, 124, 130, 133, 134, 142, 143, 148, 149, 163, 177, 179, 186, 187, 188, 190
Petroleum 209
Pets **205–11**
Phytolacca 192, 200, 201, 202, 210
Piles *see* Haemorrhoids
Phosphorus 37, 64, **89–91**, 120, 121, 140, 146, 208, 209
Podophyllum **91–3**, 146, 208
Post nasal discharge *see* Sinus and Catarrh
Pregnancy *see* Women's ailments
Premenstrual syndrome *see* Women's ailments
Pulsatilla 7, 26, 30, 31, 37, 43, 46, 68, 74, **93–5**, 102, 127, 129, 130, 135–6, 140, 147, 149, 150–1, 155, 159, 164, 173, 187, 195, 200, 201, 202, 203, 208, 209

R
Reaction, lack of 60
Rescue remedy 185, 202, 210
Restlessness *see* Emotional states
Rheumatism *see* Arthritis
Rhus tox 7, 9, 32, 48, **96–9**, 100, 128, 136, 176, 179, 193, 201, 203, 207
Ruta **99–100**, 114, 179, 201, 203, 210

S
Sabadilla 169
Sanguinaria 195
Sciatica 63, 72, 153
Sepia 195, 201, 202, 203, 210
Shock *see* Emotional states
Silicea 88, **101–3**, 117, 123, 151, 155, 169, 179, 188, 192, 202, 206, 210

Sinusitis and Catarrh 33,
36, 64, 69, 70, 71,
76, 77, 78, 79, 83,
84, 95, 102, 103, 134,
172, **186–9**
Skin disorders 28, 34, 35, 36,
45, 53, 56, 57, 70, 96, 129,
193, 195
Sleeplessness *see* Insomnia
Sneezing 44, 68, 76, 83, 85,
126, 135, 136, 167, 168, 169,
176, 186, 187, 188
Splinters *see* Injuries
Spongia 70, **103–5**, 113, 141
Sprains and Strains *see* Injuries
Staphysagria 6, 117, 155
Stings *see* Bites
Styes *see* Eye styes
Sulphur 28, 128, 130, 147, 209
Sunburn 47, 57, 58, 107,
124, 178
Sunstroke 52, 53, 69, 124
Surgery, post 43, 48, 49, 56,
177, 178
Swelling 45, 46, 47, 54, 107,
111, 116, 120, 130, 186,
193, 194
Symphytum 72, 80, **105–6**,
161, 179

T

Teething 60, 62, 92, **126–7**,
145, 149, 153
Throat, sore 34, 47, 53, 56,
70, 71, 74, 78, 83, 84, 88,
89, 101, 102, 103, 104,
130, 135, 136, 137, 149,
150, **189–92** *see
also* Laryngitis
Tics 74, 75
Tonsillitis *see* Throats, sore
Toothache *see* Mouth ulcers
and dental problems
Trifolium pratense 196

U

Ulcers, general 56, 77, 83, 84,
105, 106
Urtica **106–7**, 116, 117, 120,
125, 128, 167, 180, 193, 201,
202, 207

Urticaria 45, 46, 47, 85, 86,
98, 106, 107, 116, 117,
136, 167, **193–4**

V

Vaccinations, effects of 80,
127, 131
Verbena officinalis 196
Vertigo 54, 55, 69, 133
Vitex agnus castus 196
Viral infections *see* Colds
and Flu
Vomiting *see* Digestive disorders

W

Warts *see* Skin disorders
Weakness 48, 49, 50,
51, 66, 67, 82, 83,
133, 134, 143, 145, 146,
154, 165, 166, 169, 175,
176, 191
Whooping cough 139
Women's ailments **194–203**
Breasts
Breasts engorged 198,
200, 201
Injuries to breast tissue *see*
Injuries
Mastitis 202
Milk insufficient 107, 196,
201, 202
Nipples cracked and sore
200, 201, 202
Childbirth *see* Women's
ailments, Pregnancy
Menopause **194–5**
Menses (menstruation) 61,
62, 63, 74, 75, 81, 89, 119,
143, 144, 147, 170, 194,
195, **197**
Pregnancy 29, 128, **197–203**
Abdominal pains or pains
in the groin caused by
large or over-active baby
197, 198, 199, 201
Anxiety and Fear 197, 199,
200, 202
Baby Blues 201, 203
Baby, death, injury or
abnormality 128, 202
Bleeding 197

Braxton Hicks contractions
199, 201
Breasts *see* Women's
ailments, Breasts
Breech position — to turn
baby 200, 202
Childbirth 48, 49, 56, 72,
178, 197, 198
Constipation 202
Cramps 202
Cystitis *see* Bladder
infections
Depression 197, 203
Drugged effect after labour
as consequence of
medication 202
Haemorrhoids 203
Hair loss after
childbirth 202
Headaches 197
Indigestion and
Heartburn 202
Injuries during childbirth
198, 202
Insomnia 202
Irritability and Anger 198,
199, 203
Involuntary urination 202
Labour pain 198, 199, 202
Mood changes 202–3
Nausea and Morning-
sickness 203
Stretching of ligaments
of uterus 198, 201, 203,
Weepiness 200, 203
Premenstrual syndrome 94,
95, 154, 155, 195, 196
Wounds *see* Injuries